£2.50.

D1588719

Richard Bell's
BRITAIN

A bee-mimic; it has no
pollen baskets and the fact
that it has only one pair
of wings gives it away as
a fly. Settled down in the
yellow tray of my water
colours.

Rose bay willow herb.

Richard Bell's
BRITAIN

COLLINS
St James's Place, London

For Barbara, who often sent me packing
and occasionally joined me on the road.

William Collins Sons & Co Ltd
London Glasgow Sydney Auckland
Toronto Johannesburg

First published 1981
© Richard Bell 1981

ISBN 0 00 219569 0

Colour reproduction by Adroit Photo Litho Ltd, Birmingham
Filmset by Jolly & Barber Ltd, Rugby
Printed and bound by William Collins Sons & Co Ltd, Glasgow

Acknowledgments

Exploring Britain can be lonely, but my year's journey gave me an opportunity to visit friends and relations who are scattered about the country. It was pleasant to be able to work alone in the fields all day and then to enjoy conversation, catching up on news and a meal with friends in the evening . . . the best of both worlds. So I have a lot of people to thank for encouragement, hot dinners and a bed for the night.

Including: Jim and Rosamund Horton, Jeremy Galton, Erol Bryant, Vanessa Clegg, Elizabeth Butterworth, Christopher and Doreen Reynolds, Jackie Atkinson, Andrew Wyllie, Adrian and Pamela Littlewood, Christopher and Kathy Sampson, Sylvia Smith, Mr and Mrs Pascoe, Julie and John Norris Wood, Tony and Jutta Manser, Roger and Joyce Carpenter, Joyce Parker, Tony and Judy Dale, Hilda and Maurice Smith, Mrs Williams, John Williams, Rhian Deiniolen and her parents, David and Hilary Stubbs, Carol and David Pemberton, John Busby, Linda and David Ingham and, at base camp, I would like to thank my parents, my girlfriend Barbara and her parents for making my fleeting visits home so pleasant. Having toured the whole of Britain I can confirm that the best Yorkshire puddings are made in Yorkshire.

Contents

Kestrels use the corners of the mill's roof as vantage points. They are showing an interest in the nest in the sycamore to the right of the mill. One sat in the nest calling while the other bird circled. They would suddenly swoop low over walls as if trying to catch starlings unawares.

Hogweed and nettles pushed their way up through concrete rubble.

Hygromia striolata

Dock leaves unfurling amongst last year's canes.

Racing
Pigeons

INTRODUCTION

Britain is rich in scenery and wildlife, few parts of the world contain such
a variety of landscape in so small an area. My journey took me to
highlands and islands, fenland, woods and heaths, rivers, canals, old
industrial sites, estuaries and coastlines. An exploration that took the form
of a clockwise tour around England, Wales and Scotland, starting at my
own doorstep in Yorkshire in July and finishing there a year later. Each
acre that I visited had something different to offer; each acre was unique.
If you tread softly and keep your eyes and ears open there is always
something new to see, even in the most familiar territory: coots battling
on flooded pastures; a migrant wader moving along the water's edge like a
clockwork toy; ants collecting honeydew from aphids on a stem of tansy,
a kestrel perched on a chimney.

When I began this book my first idea was to concentrate on some
appropriate theme at each place I visited. After only a few expeditions,
however, it became clear that if I spent the time looking for textbook
examples of botany or geology I would miss the spontaneous and
unexpected events that make the country so refreshing and enjoyable.
So my aim here has been to give something of the flavour of a particular
place on a particular day. A day in the country isn't something you can
plan; it's an unpredictable series of incidents, sights, sounds and smells.
There will always be a few surprises.

I went out to do a watercolour of Crab Bay. This is the result. I spilt the water and was distracted by a seal (on the right ↗) which swam into the Bay.

Sketchbook of a visit to Skokholm island during Easter 1970. Ten years later I returned to the island and drew again at Crab Bay (see page 128).

10

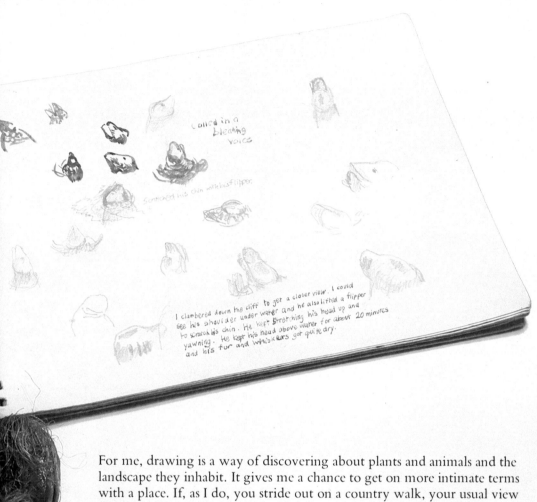

Called in a bleating voice

Scratched his chin with his flipper.

I clambered down the cliff to get a closer view. I could see his shoulder under water and he also lifted a flipper to scratch his chin. He kept stretching his head up and yawning. He kept his head above water for about 20 minutes and his fur and whiskers got quite dry.

For me, drawing is a way of discovering about plants and animals and the landscape they inhabit. It gives me a chance to get on more intimate terms with a place. If, as I do, you stride out on a country walk, your usual view of a bird will be of it flying away, but when I sit drawing hawthorn blossom, for example, warblers and other small birds will hop into the branches close by me. (When I was drawing magpies in London Zoo I was most surprised when a voice asked 'What are you doing?' I didn't realise magpies could speak with such uncanny human intonation, though I think only orang-utans truly appreciate my artwork.) I've been sworn at by grey squirrels in beechwoods and pelted with pine cones by a red squirrel. When I'm sitting quietly I can actually *see* a water vole instead of just hearing the plop as it swims away. Even the unlikeliest spot, if you look carefully enough, is bustling with life.

I got into the habit of keeping a sketchbook ten years ago during a visit to Skokholm island, off the coast of south Wales near Milford Haven. Isolated and unspoilt, the wilderness of Skokholm is rich in plant and animal life and for a fortnight that Easter I was able to immerse myself completely in observing and drawing the life around me. Free from the pace and pressures of everyday life, that first visit to Skokholm gave me a rare opportunity. It taught me the value of giving my undivided attention to nature. What matters is to be open to everything going on around you, whether you are looking at the tilted strata in a sea cliff or at a small patch

The weasel's bounding forays were punctuated by quizzical surveys. The mixture of cover and open spaces in a marginal place like this must suit an opportunist ambusher. Later I surprised it up on the bridge and it backed away into a trackside hole, perhaps it had a run and a nest hole inside the framework.

Black spleenwort in a crevice between the sandstone blocks of the bridge piers.

The box-girder construction of the bridge reminded me of the inner structure of bullrushes. As I broke this piece off (which took some doing) from a plant in the marshy field by the bridge I set up a rabbit. It raced down the track and I was afraid I would have rabbit footprints over this page, but when it go to my bottle of ink it changed course and leapt a foot in the air.
... I think that might confuse a weasel following a scent trail.

The diagonal struts that brace the coat-hanger shaped sides of the bridge get thinner towards the middle of the bridge, where presumably there is less stress. Such subtlety of design comes from a practical respect for the laws of nature rather than a stylish whim on the part of the designer. There is a similar theme in the design of the fern leaf.

of deep yellow lichen on a salt-splashed rock. For instance, as I was painting the view of Crab Bay on Skokholm shown above, I was side-tracked by the presence of a seal. But far from being a distraction, the seal is a vital part of the island scene. It gives some animation to the drawing and ecologically it belongs there because it comes at the end of many sea-shore food chains.

What is true of wild places is also true of the countryside nearer home. Animals and birds are a living expression of the landscape that supports them. Directly or indirectly they all rely on plants for food and the plants in turn are dependent on the opportunities offered by nature and by man. Tumbling brambles, docks, grasses, broom and elder soften the outline of the masonry of the railway bridge. Besides providing food for the rabbits they give cover to a hunting weasel. The rabbits that feed in the marshy field have bolt holes close by in the dry railway embankment, amongst the brambles and elder.

Plants and animals take advantage of man's activities. Indeed, it is difficult to understand the wildlife of most places without considering what man has done there. But these human activities still depend on the natural potential of an area. For instance, the railway and the canal it crosses are both used for carrying coal. The sandstone used in the bridge was laid down in vast deltas at a time when giant club mosses and fern-like trees (distant relatives of the ferns and mosses that grow on the bridge today) grew in the dense forests that were to be transformed into coal.

So if you are watching wildlife it is useful to know something about the history of an area and also about its prehistory. Everything is interrelated. I have even extended my interests to astronomy because I feel that an understanding of what goes on in the universe gives a fresh perspective to a look at a small part of the Earth's surface.

But the key subject is geology. The country is made up of layer upon layer of history that can be read like a book . . . a very battered and crumpled book with many pages missing. As you learn a little about our island's journey through time, reading the landscape becomes addictive. Shapes and contours begin to emerge that you would not otherwise have noticed – they would not have meant anything. The three-dimensional countryside takes on the extra dimension of time. But the more one learns the more mysteries present themselves. The theory of continental drift has thrown new light on events in the distant past that have left Britain's fabric wrinkled, creased and ragged at the edges.

For a book which is intended to reflect Britain through the seasons there is one omission that will soon become apparent – I haven't included any snow scenes. I must confess that I'm very fond of creature comforts and I decided early on that the purpose of being out in the field was to look and draw, not to prove how tough I am by braving ice and snow. So at Christmas I took time off to celebrate and to identify the plants and animals I had sketched on the first half of my expedition.

I have been out in the snow on a few occasions, however. During the previous winter I spent a day at Malham in Yorkshire. The bus driver warned me on the way that 'there's nowat up there, only snow'; it had taken over the landscape, covering the hills and gathering into deep drifts along dry-stone walls. There was a layer of soft, powdery snow on the fields around the village but most of the drifts had an inch of hard crust, in places rippled by the wind to give a sharp-edged fluting effect. It's always very quiet out there, and the snow and the stillness of the day made it seem even quieter. As I walked on up the valley I could hear a shepherd on the other side whistling his dog. The silence was so complete that I was aware of the sound of my own footsteps; it was like being in a cool, quiet cathedral.

The stillness made it quite comfortable to work in the low winter sunshine, but the day was colder than it seemed. The watercolour turned to ice crystals the moment I put it on the paper, like damp washing instantly going stiff when hung out on a cold day. This was most disconcerting and made work difficult. As you can see, when I got back to my bed and breakfast the iced watercolour melted and the ink ran.

Malham,
January.

A Smuggler's tea-shoppe in Whitby, but this one did seem genuine, there was a narrow cobbled alley-way outside and it had such a low entrance that I cracked my head as I came in.

Another weekend that winter I went to Whitby. Snow was settling on the beach and I spent most of the time touring the teashops – after a year's journey around Britain I could write a book on teashops. I drew views from the youth hostel, from under a concrete platform and finally from a telephone box overlooking the fish quay. Afterwards I visited Whitby Abbey. Sheltering in those deserted ruins, with a freezing wind over the headland and fragments of ice jingling in the pond, I could easily imagine the isolation and simplicity of abbey life. But my attention was soon claimed by a caterpillar of brightly coloured anoraks making an even faster than usual lightning tour in order to beat the oncoming snow.

There are a lot of question marks in this book and I would have put in even more, except that I felt it would become monotonous. Certain groups of plants and animals are difficult to identify, even for specialists. But I was determined to try. It would be a pity to ignore certain creatures and plants just because you can't find a name for them, or miss out on geology because the subject seems too complex to grasp. All these things add interest and enjoyment to a walk in the country.

Richard Bell, January 1981

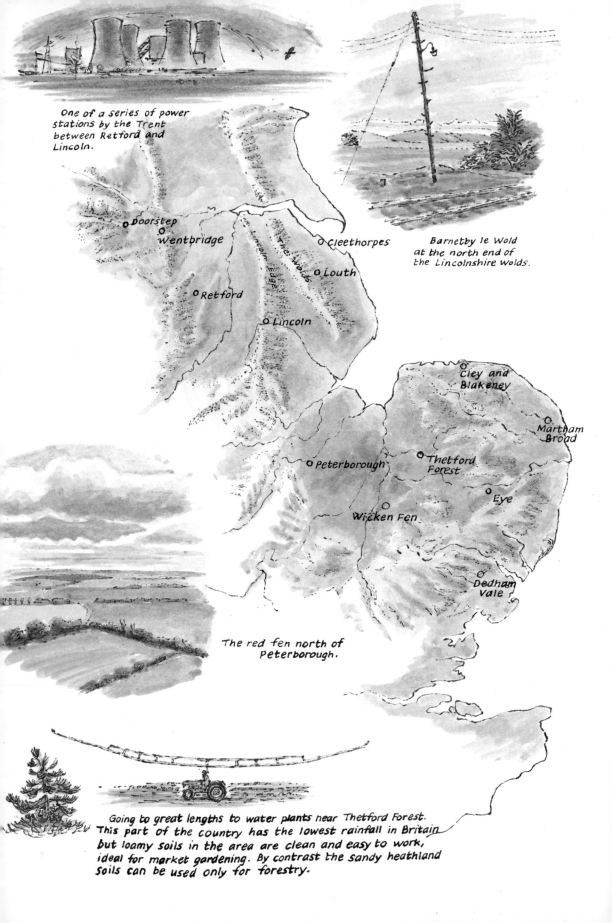

One of a series of power stations by the Trent between Retford and Lincoln.

Barnetby le Wold at the north end of the Lincolnshire wolds.

Doorstep
Wentbridge
Cleethorpes
The Wolds
Louth
Lincoln Edge
Retford
Lincoln

Cley and Blakeney
Martham Broad
Peterborough
Thetford Forest
Eye
Wicken Fen
Dedham Vale

The red fen north of Peterborough.

Going to great lengths to water plants near Thetford Forest. This part of the country has the lowest rainfall in Britain but loamy soils in the area are clean and easy to work, ideal for market gardening. By contrast the sandy heathland soils can be used only for forestry.

EASTERN ENGLAND

July

By sitting and watching carefully I soon realised that I could fill a whole sketchbook with observations just of my front doorstep near Wakefield. Plants grow up in corners, flies bask in the sun, spiders spin webs while at night slugs, woodlice and centipedes come out from the protection of crevices. There are innumerable things to record. 'Doesn't it worry you that if you stopped to look carefully at everything you'd never get further than the front doorstep?' a friend asked me. No, it doesn't really worry me. I'm not attempting to compile a complete catalogue of everything that can be seen. It is the quality of observation that is important rather than the quantity, what you see rather than how much.

Even in a well-known place there are still fresh discoveries to be made. Lincoln, for example, is seething with history. Visitors to the city climb medieval thoroughfares up to the cathedral, with its imposing gateway and the castle near by. With the help of a guide book you can understand the development of the town from Roman times. Most people who tackle the cathedral with watercolours would probably show it in this historical setting, framed by timbered buildings and stone archways. But look a bit closer. It turns out that this magnificent pile of a building is entirely composed of fossil remains from a warm prehistoric sea. This is why I drew the cathedral from about three feet; visitors must have thought I was a very short-sighted illustrator.

The line of Lincoln Edge continues diagonally southwest across England through Northamptonshire and Edge Hill to the Cotswolds. On my travels I've taken this scarp as a dividing line: to the west are the industrial Midlands and to the east the lonely fens. Rocks and soils seem to affect not only industry but also local character. As I made my way by bus and train the accents changed. The Suffolk dialect, for example, seems to grow directly from the soil.

Some way to the southeast of this scarp lies Peterborough, set on a flat expanse of fenland. In contrast to Lincoln's spectacularly positioned cathedral, Peterborough's is hemmed about by the town. But it was the brickpits here that caught my attention; they proved to be one of the most surprising places I visited. With ranks of tall chimneys and yawning holes, this is an extreme example of the effects of industrial activity on the land. Yet I discovered that the derelict ground had become virtually an unofficial nature reserve, rich in wild flowers, attracting butterflies, damselflies and other insects, birds and mammals. High speed trains rush through these brickyards on the main line to Kings Cross, and if you take a rail journey along this route you can see how the fens change colour. North of Peterborough the land is red while to the south the line crosses an expanse of black fen. On an overcast day this flat, featureless land can be dark and brooding, dissected by a shining geometry of dykes. But there is one patch of colour as the line goes through Wood Walton nature reserve a few miles south of Peterborough, an extensive stand of silver birch that flashes white against the black of the surrounding country.

At Cley next the Sea there is a very different kind of nature reserve which has become a Mecca for birdwatchers. Here I saw avocets for the first time and was particularly delighted to see a spoonbill. This is organised birdwatching at its best, with a spacious hide, controlled water levels and screens erected to allow access without disturbing the birds. But with about twenty people in the hide the excitement of this was dampened for me; on the other hand, the experienced birdwatchers there pointed out distant birds I would otherwise have missed.

In most places it is good to do no more than sit quietly and watch, but at Cley I was also committed to some walking. If you want to explore the area you have to walk right along the shingle spit to where the boat for Blakeney will pick you up, or else turn back the way you came. In the Middle Ages Cley was an important harbour, but now the shingle ridge separates it from the sea and the marsh that has formed behind the ridge is where you go birdwatching. The shingle spit and the dunes leading to it are features the sea has constructed.

When I was at Eye I visited Dunwich where, in contrast to Cley, the sea is very much in evidence as a destructive force. I'd cycled there with some friends and as we arrived a sudden thunderstorm broke. A child was killed by lightning on a beach farther up the coast. In medieval times Dunwich was a prosperous port, but during a violent storm the sea broke through the shingle bar that protected the harbour and steady erosion followed. Now the old port has disappeared and all that remains of the town's churchyard is a single grave.

Coastal erosion is rapid because the rocks are young and soft. In East Anglia sands, gravel and the peat of the Broads and the fen country blanket older, harder rocks. At Thetford Forest the soils are sandy and the rainfall is low, so that this is the nearest thing to a desert you can find in

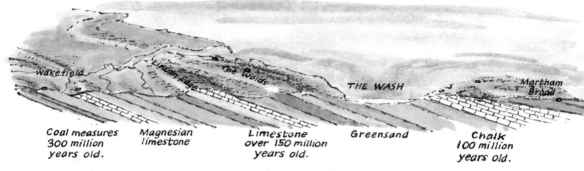

Coal measures   Magnesian   Limestone   Greensand   Chalk
300 million   limestone   over 150 million   100 million
years old.   years old.   years old.

Slice across eastern England from Wakefield to Martham Broad to show how harder rocks such as limestones give rise to landscape features.

Britain. Here the underlying grain of the landscape is obscured, but at a place such as Lincoln Edge it is easy to see the dipping strata.

It is difficult to look at the lofty trees and waterside meadows of Dedham Vale without thinking of Constable's paintings. Visitors now arrive by the coachload to see Flatford Mill, made famous by the 'Haywain'. At a time when many English artists were working on fanciful Italian landscapes, Constable's paintings came as a breath of fresh air; they made people aware of what had been around them all the time. When I called at the Mill, which is now a Field Studies Centre, one group of biology students was looking at the vale in terms of graphs and coloured diagrams. They had been catching waterboatmen and marking them with blobs of white paint as part of a population survey. This is valuable scientific groundwork, though in my view the results should be taken with a pinch of salt . . . numbers tend to take on a magical significance and nature is always more subtle than the numbers suggest.

I asked their teacher if she could help me to identify a water beetle I'd drawn. 'You can't be all that bothered about an accurate identification,' she replied, 'or you'd have brought the beetle back with you.' I expect that is true, but if I brought back everything I drew I'd have buckets full of specimens by now. Wild plants and animals have enough to put up with, without me collecting and killing as I go.

Shorter tailed young in the large beech.

Magpie standing Sentinel. Their ratchet-Screwdriver call funnels down the chimney and out of my fireplace.

LIME WASHED OUT FROM MORTAR.

Doorstep
Wakefield, Yorkshire, July

'A thousand mile journey begins with one step.'

It seems appropriate to start this journey round Britain with a closer look at very familiar home ground. Here is just a selection of wildlife around the front doorstep, I could have filled pages with observations. We've had hedgehogs, collared doves, wood pigeons, tawny owls, two grey squirrels and even a bat in the garden this year. Victorian shrubberies provide shelter and some food for birds and other creatures.

There is so much to choose from that knowing where to start is a problem. But I could start, for instance, with that one brick, eroded by rain, frost and wind to show shaly fragments. The local mudstone that it was made from was laid down some 300 million years ago when this part of the earth's surface was part of a vast delta. Britain was then near the equator and luxuriant coal forest grew on mudbanks. The sandstone that the steps are cut from was laid down at this time in faster flowing water. The remains of the coal forests helped fuel the industrial revolution, hence the black scum on the bricks and sandstone, representing 100 years of progress.

Sulphur dioxide gets into the air when coal and other fossil fuels are burnt. The rain falls as dilute sulphurous acid. To make matters worse rocks around here don't have enough lime in them to counteract this acidity. Certain plants can't survive here (such as those I drew on the limestone at Wentbridge, shown on the next spread). Lichens in particular fare badly and there aren't any on the acidic sandstone steps or on the bricks.

Blackbird, wings fanned out over the ground, sunning itself.

Honey coloured humble-bee visiting the aubretia. Small, light manoeuvres, not the debris-scattering hovercraft hover of the larger bumble bees.

Both large and small white butterflies and various hoverflies come to the aubretia

Cladonia fimbriata (?)

Just to the left of the steps on the rockery there is a colony of Cladonia lichen. I think the rock it is growing on is slag from a blast furnace with a touch of limestone flux in it.

The air is getting cleaner; it probably would not have survived 10 or 15 years ago,

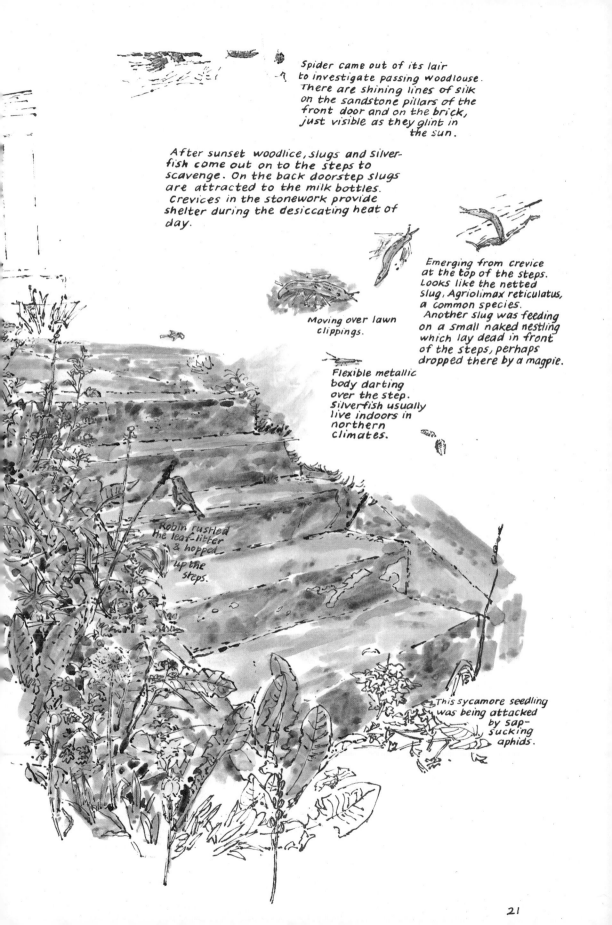

Spider came out of its lair to investigate passing woodlouse. There are shining lines of silk on the sandstone pillars of the front door and on the brick, just visible as they glint in the sun.

After sunset woodlice, slugs and silverfish come out on to the steps to scavenge. On the back doorstep slugs are attracted to the milk bottles. Crevices in the stonework provide shelter during the desiccating heat of day.

Moving over lawn clippings.

Emerging from crevice at the top of the steps. Looks like the netted slug, Agriolimax reticulatus, a common species.
Another slug was feeding on a small naked nestling which lay dead in front of the steps, perhaps dropped there by a magpie.

Flexible metallic body darting over the step. Silverfish usually live indoors in northern climates.

Robin rustled the leaf-litter & hopped up the steps.

This sycamore seedling was being attacked by sap-sucking aphids.

The railway viaduct over the little River Went marks the eastern edge of the area of country around Wakefield that I have been studying for the past eight years. It is an area of coal age shales with sandstone escarpment. When I walked out to this bridge I looked out to the scarp of Magnesian limestone, just outside my frame of reference.

Now that I have the opportunity I'd like to look at the plants of the limestone and see which are different from the plants of coal measures soils.

Black Bryony

I've never before seen clover forming a three foot high hedge so I started drawing it. No it isn't a luxuriant specialised limestone plant, a local lady told me, it is Lucerne clover, they harvest it three times a year. This narrow strip along the field edge hadn't been harvested as at the time it was still recovering from vehicles going over it during the snows.

White Bryony very abundant in the hedges.

Both the Bryonies are at the northern edge of their range here and they seem to do best on the limestone.

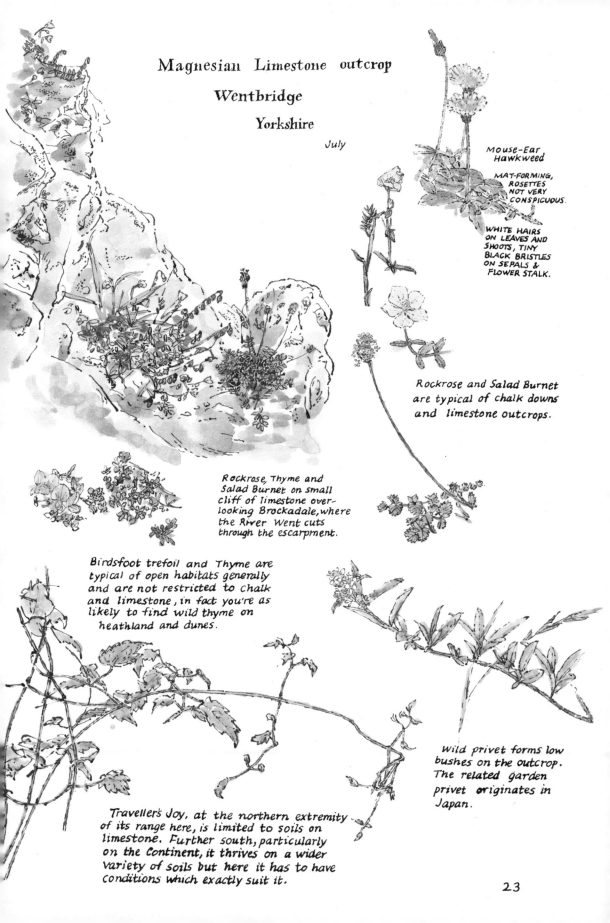

Magnesian Limestone outcrop
Wentbridge
Yorkshire

July

Mouse-Ear Hawkweed

MAT-FORMING, ROSETTES NOT VERY CONSPICUOUS.

WHITE HAIRS ON LEAVES AND SHOOTS, TINY BLACK BRISTLES ON SEPALS & FLOWER STALK.

Rockrose and Salad Burnet are typical of chalk downs and limestone outcrops.

Rockrose, Thyme and Salad Burnet on small cliff of limestone overlooking Brockadale, where the River Went cuts through the escarpment.

Birdsfoot trefoil and Thyme are typical of open habitats generally and are not restricted to chalk and limestone, in fact you're as likely to find wild thyme on heathland and dunes.

Wild privet forms low bushes on the outcrop. The related garden privet originates in Japan.

Traveller's Joy, at the northern extremity of its range here, is limited to soils on limestone. Further south, particularly on the Continent, it thrives on a wider variety of soils but here it has to have conditions which exactly suit it.

Gravel Pit, Retford

Two great crested grebes were fighting, beaks interlocked... they submerged.

One went back to the stripy headed young and greeted its mate by extending crest and cheek feathers and arching its neck.

Pair of tattered lapwings.

Mute swan floating by like a cumulus cloud, resting its neck.

A pair of coots keep diving and feeding their six young.

Coot making a duck feel unwelcome.

Brown butterfly

Heads held upright like a knight in chess, wings outspread heraldically for balance. Thrashing violently with legs.

Threat display, a dispute between the coots with young and another pair. A jet fighter thundered across; another form of territorial imperative, but when it comes to aggression coots have the edge on us.

A swan was gracefully dipping and coming up with a bill of what looked like strands of algae. For one awful moment I thought it was tangled in fishing line, but it was only a strand of algae draped over its shoulder.

There were lots of pebbles of quartzite around. Quartzite is sandstone altered by heat and pressure. There aren't any volcanic or metamorphic rocks nearby so, I wondered, were the pebbles brought here by glaciers from Scotland or Scandinavia?
No, the geological map says the gravel beds are alluvial not glacial. The river had eroded ready-made pebbles from the local Bunter Pebble beds; these beds are debris washed down into temporary lakes from a desert to the south or west some 225 million years ago. So the quartzite pebbles must come from metamorphic rocks to the south west... from around Dartmoor or Wales?

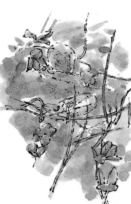

The soils here are sandy and reddish; a reminder of the hot desert conditions at the time when the Bunter Pebble beds were laid down.

24

Froghopper
with 2 foot hop

Two of the gravel pits have
been banked around and are used
for dumping the fine fly ash from
the large power stations that are
prominent landmarks in this lowland
countryside. At places along the edge
of the lagoon, especially in this
corner, willows and some reedmace
have colonised the ashy silt.

A pair of reed
buntings flew along
the willows.

Aphids

Orangey brown
skipper butterfly,
whir of wings as
it took off.
Must have
been the small
skipper, the
caterpillars
feed on grass.

Out of the selection of hawkweeds
illustrated by Keble Martin in the
Concise Flora this most nearly
resembles Hieracium vulgatum,
even to the tendency of the leaves
to turn beetroot coloured. Plentiful
on the dry grassy embankment
of the lagoon.

Tufted vetch in full
flower scrambling
amongst the grasses

25

Lincoln Edge   July

SCARP SLOPE   DIP SLOPE

The limestone is more resistant to weathering than the clays and sands it rests on.

This view from South common gives a profile of the escarpment of Lincoln Edge. The cathedral is built of limestone quarried from the hill on which it stands.

Some of the blocks contain shell fragments in large numbers. And there are spindle and bullet-shaped remains of other invertebrate creatures that lived in the tropical Jurassic seas of 150 million years ago. Their shapes are scattered about the blocks like the floating forms of Paul Klee's paintings.

It seems odd to make a drawing of a medieval cathedral from only three feet away but today my interest is in the prehistoric rather than the historic.

BELEMNITE & SHELL. THE SHELL RETAINED A MOTHER OF PEARL EFFECT.

The stone of the pillars on the west side is crammed full of small fossil shells. The stone must be rich in iron, it has turned a rusty colour but is grey where chipped away.

Tiny white bivalve shell embedded in the mortar, not fossilised

Belemnites are the equivalent of the Cuttlefish of modern squids; an internal shell that serves as a skeleton.

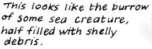

This looks like the burrow of some sea creature, half filled with shelly debris.

26

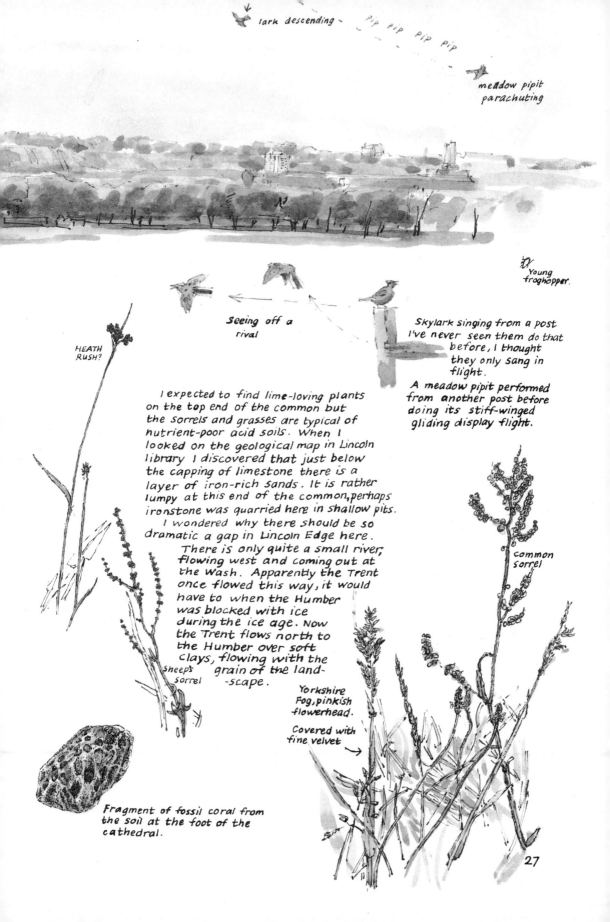

lark descending

Pip Pip Pip Pip Pip

meadow pipit
parachuting

Young
froghopper.

Seeing off a
rival

HEATH
RUSH?

Skylark singing from a post
I've never seen them do that
before, I thought
they only sang in
flight.

A meadow pipit performed
from another post before
doing its stiff-winged
gliding display flight.

I expected to find lime-loving plants
on the top end of the common but
the sorrels and grasses are typical of
nutrient-poor acid soils. When I
looked on the geological map in Lincoln
library I discovered that just below
the capping of limestone there is a
layer of iron-rich sands. It is rather
lumpy at this end of the common, perhaps
ironstone was quarried here in shallow pits.
    I wondered why there should be so
dramatic a gap in Lincoln Edge here.
    There is only quite a small river,
flowing west and coming out at
the Wash. Apparently the Trent
once flowed this way, it would
have to when the Humber
was blocked with ice
during the ice age. Now
the Trent flows north to
the Humber over soft
clays, flowing with the
grain of the land-
-scape.

common
sorrel

Sheep's
sorrel

Yorkshire
Fog, pinkish
flowerhead.

Covered with
fine velvet →

Fragment of fossil coral from
the soil at the foot of the
cathedral.

27

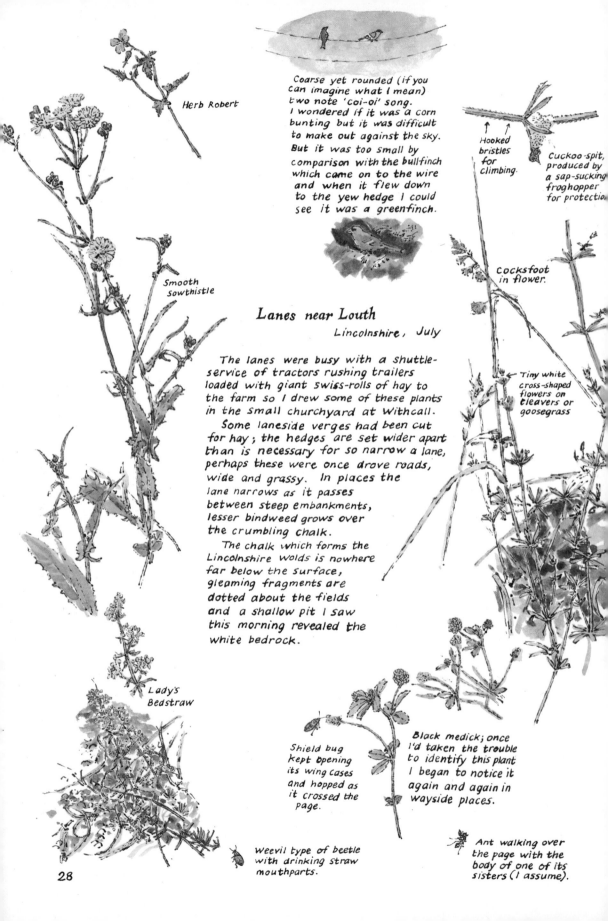

Herb Robert

Coarse yet rounded (if you
can imagine what I mean)
two note 'coi-oi' song.
I wondered if it was a corn
bunting but it was difficult
to make out against the sky.
But it was too small by
comparison with the bullfinch
which came on to the wire
and when it flew down
to the yew hedge I could
see it was a greenfinch.

Hooked
bristles
for
climbing.

Cuckoo-spit,
produced by
a sap-sucking
froghopper
for protection

Cocksfoot
in flower.

Smooth
Sowthistle

Lanes near Louth

Lincolnshire, July

The lanes were busy with a shuttle-
service of tractors rushing trailers
loaded with giant swiss-rolls of hay to
the farm so I drew some of these plants
in the small churchyard at Withcall.
   Some laneside verges had been cut
for hay; the hedges are set wider apart
than is necessary for so narrow a lane,
perhaps these were once drove roads,
wide and grassy. In places the
lane narrows as it passes
between steep embankments,
lesser bindweed grows over
the crumbling chalk.
   The chalk which forms the
Lincolnshire Wolds is nowhere
far below the surface,
gleaming fragments are
dotted about the fields
and a shallow pit I saw
this morning revealed the
white bedrock.

Tiny white
cross-shaped
flowers on
cleavers or
goosegrass

Lady's
Bedstraw

Shield bug
kept opening
its wing cases
and hopped as
it crossed the
page.

Black medick; once
I'd taken the trouble
to identify this plant
I began to notice it
again and again in
wayside places.

Weevil type of beetle
with drinking straw
mouthparts.

Ant walking over
the page with the
body of one of its
sisters (I assume).

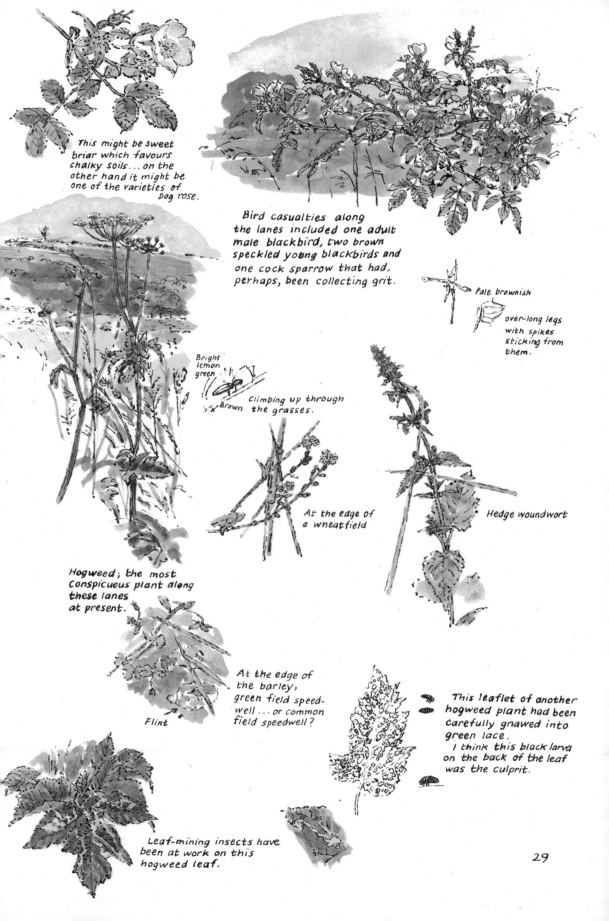

This might be sweet briar which favours chalky soils... on the other hand it might be one of the varieties of Dog rose.

Bird casualties along the lanes included one adult male blackbird, two brown speckled young blackbirds and one cock sparrow that had, perhaps, been collecting grit.

Pale brownish

over-long legs with spikes sticking from them.

Bright lemon green

Brown

Climbing up through the grasses.

At the edge of a wheatfield

Hedge woundwort

Hogweed; the most conspicuous plant along these lanes at present.

Flint

At the edge of the barley, green field speedwell... or common field speedwell?

This leaflet of another hogweed plant had been carefully gnawed into green lace.
I think this black larva on the back of the leaf was the culprit.

Leaf-mining insects have been at work on this hogweed leaf.

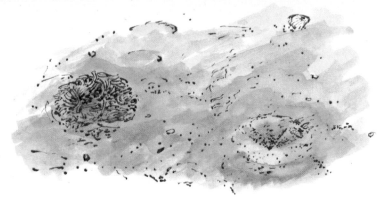

There were thousands, perhaps millions, of casts of lugworms on the beach. Every cast is connected by a U-shaped tunnel to a funnel-shaped hollow where more material is drawn in.

Beachcombing at Cleethorpes

July

Spurn head just visible in the mist at the other side of the Humber. Perhaps I'll be able to visit it on my return trip... if winter gales leave it intact.

Common periwinkles on chalk boulder.

Broken whelk shell with blob of black oil inside it.

Barnacles on cockle shell.

Common or Edible mussel.

Hornwrack, each of the holes in the flattened fronds held a filter-feeding animal.

Common whelk; the notch at the front of the shell is for a siphon tube.
The whelk uses the tube for searching out carrion-dead fish and crabs and suchlike-underwater.

Razor shell

Rayed trough shell.

Piddock-the file-like ridges at the front end enable it to burrow into chalk and other soft rocks.

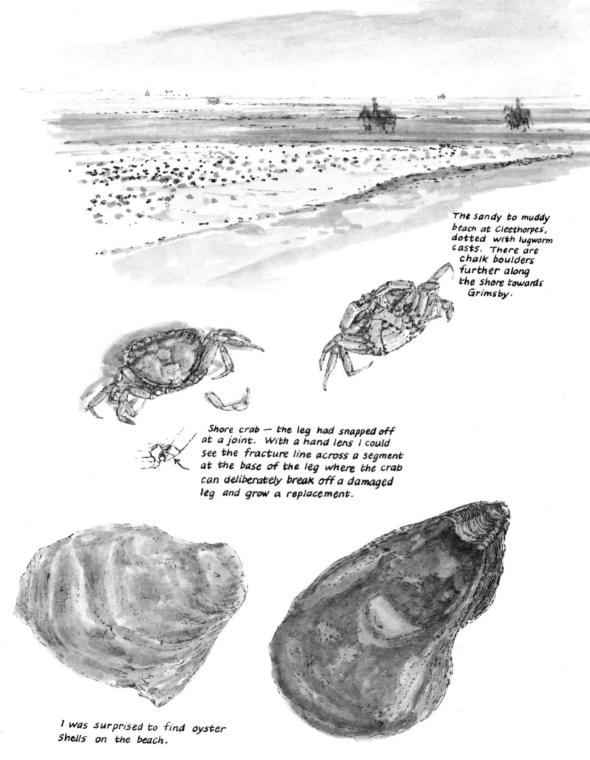

The sandy to muddy beach at Cleethorpes, dotted with lugworm casts. There are chalk boulders further along the shore towards Grimsby.

Shore crab — the leg had snapped off at a joint. With a hand lens I could see the fracture line across a segment at the base of the leg where the crab can deliberately break off a damaged leg and grow a replacement.

I was surprised to find oyster shells on the beach.

Marsh
thistle

Wicken Fen

Cambridgeshire   July

Reeds for thatching were cut here. Reedbeds that have been left uncut have been
taken over by dense thickets of willow and
alder known as carr. A group of conservation
volunteers were busy cutting back an area
of carr to give the reeds and marsh plants
an opportunity.

Who should I meet in the pub at lunchtime
but Eric Simms. He's currently working on
a book about warblers so I asked him, just
what is the difference between the songs of
the sedge and reed warblers?

The sedge warblers gave an extraordinary
performance, a sound collage of harsh croaks and
musical notes interspersed with snippets of
impressions of other birds. In some parts of
the reserve there was one every 10 or 20 yards
in willows very close to the path.

The reed warbler tends to be a shier bird.
The song doesn't go so high or so low as that
of the sedge warbler, nor does it carry so far.

Meadow rue

Early marsh
orchid.

Yellow loosestrife.
As I sat on the ground
drawing three people
walked by. The ground
shook as the black
peat vibrated.

Alder buckthorn, a shrub, growing with willows at the edge of the sedge fen.

The marsh pea proved a restless model; the whole reedbed was shaken by the wind.

The temperature was almost in the eighties and biting insects were particularly active — there were plenty of mosquitoes and one determined horse-fly had me running two hundred yards down one of the droves.

Yellow rattle along the droves. (Droves are paths mown through the sedge fen).

Large brown dragonfly patrolling along the drove. Turning right-angles, as manoeuvrable as a helicopter.

Brushing away mosquitoes every few seconds made drawing very difficult especially as the ink kept coagulating in the heat. In desperation I resorted to putting on my thick anorak with the hood up, and even draping my pullover round my ankles. I hope no-one saw me sitting there swathed up in this sweltering heat.

My favourite of all the plants here - bog myrtle or sweet gale. It had such a fragrance.

Southern marsh orchid.

THE DAY OF THE APHIDS

My friend Jim met me at the station with two bicycles (quite an achievement, cycling across Cambridge with one bike in tow!) As we cycled back he called to me 'It's starting to rain!' But there was hardly a cloud in the sky, the rain was sap excreted by aphids feeding in the lofty lime trees. The pavement under the limes carried a permanent black shadow where sooty moulds grew on the fallen sap.

This summer there has been a terrific build up in aphid numbers. They gathered in drifts in bus windows and I shared a telephone box with several hundred of them. Total strangers would greet you in the street, 'Lot o'flies about today!' The Daily Mail ran a feature with a close-up photograph.

Though they seem so fragile and helpless as individuals, as a species they're ready to take advantage of favourable conditions, reproducing faster than ladybirds and lacewings can devour them.

33

Thetford Forest
Norfolk July

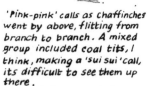

OLIVE UPPER PARTS, SOMETIMES IN PAIRS IN FLIGHT ABOVE TREE CANOPY.

'I wish these pine woods stretched on to the edge of doom, where no wheel turns the sandy track.'

Said Robert Frost in a poem,

These forest tracks lead on to the New Stone Age flint mines at Grime's Graves. I walked across the forest to get there yesterday evening. Each track and ride was different; some newly cleared some, overgrown; blue viper's bugloss, yellow fennel and mullein grew along sandy lanes, there was a smell of cut pine where trees were being thinned.

But I missed seeing the flint mines; I came out at a notice which said 'Grimes Graves Army Gun Range' and I could hear shooting in the distance.

There is so much I should like to draw but I don't want this account of Thetford Forest to be like one of those 'Greatest Hits..' records. There's more than enough to keep me occupied on this 100 yard stretch of forest track close to the Forestry Commision Brandon Depot... that is, if I look carefully. I felt too much the sight-seer, dashing about ticking off the sights I ought to see at Wicken Fen.

What is true of the Breckland as a whole should be reflected here on this particular stretch of track.

'Pink-pink' calls as chaffinches went by above, flitting from branch to branch. A mixed group included coal tits, I think, making a 'sui sui'call, its difficult to see them up there.

A flock I saw next day definitely did contain a lot of acrobatic coal tits, some great tits and at least one treecreeper.

Wren, even more bad-tempered than usual (if that is possible) chittering at me from one of the elms growing amongst the pines.

A clatter and two disputing pheasants emerged. They remind me not a little of small dinosaurs. Their bird-brained mentality. You see a handsome cock pheasant in the middle of a vast fenland field, neck in the question-mark position, apparently lost in thought... "where am I? What am I going to do next?"

Maybe this hoverfly had Viper's bugloss in mind as three times it settled on a particular blue section of the design on my thermos flask.

I was drawing this speckled brown butterfly. When I looked up it had disappeared, there was only a dried-up leaf where it had been; it had closed its wings. It was a speckled wood butterfly - what else?

There were a lot of harvestmen ambling amongst the forest floor vegetation. One was sheltering in a paper bag in my haversack, apparently unperturbed by the bottle of Citronella insect repellent oil inside (I'm taking no chances after Wicken Fen). Of course a harvestman isn't an insect; its Cornish pasty body has eight legs (ten if you include the antennae-like ones in front) nor does it have a seperate thorax and abdomen as spiders do.

ACTUALLY THERE IS A HINT OF THE DIVISION OF THE BODY

TINY BRIGHT RED EGG-LIKE OBJECT ATTACHED TO ONE OF ITS LEGS — A MITE PERHAPS

WALKING APHID

STATIONARY FROGHOPPER

There is a dark stripe on the under-side of this spider. I expect if you spend most of your life hanging upside-down it makes sense to reverse the usual guide-lines for disruptive coloration.

Spider hanging from its web, a loose filmy net slung between the grasses. It moved its legs one by one as if twanging the net to check if the reverberations revealed a trapped insect. Its slow methodical movements were broken by a rapid dash. It caught a tiny black insect which it took back to the centre.

In fact it seems most closely related to the three-legged Martian war-machines in 'War of the Worlds' which could cross difficult terrain.

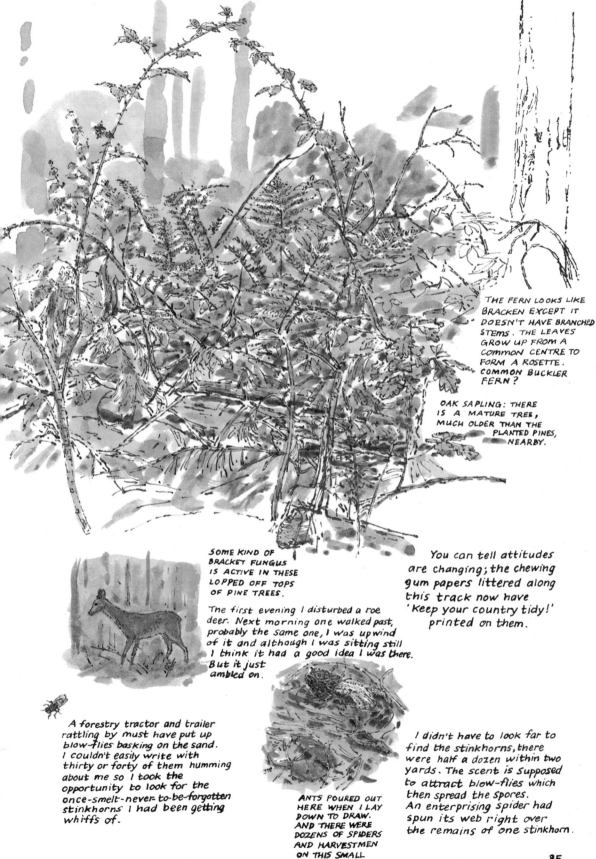

THE FERN LOOKS LIKE BRACKEN EXCEPT IT DOESN'T HAVE BRANCHED STEMS. THE LEAVES GROW UP FROM A COMMON CENTRE TO FORM A ROSETTE. COMMON BUCKLER FERN?

OAK SAPLING: THERE IS A MATURE TREE, MUCH OLDER THAN THE PLANTED PINES, NEARBY.

SOME KIND OF BRACKET FUNGUS IS ACTIVE IN THESE LOPPED OFF TOPS OF PINE TREES.

The first evening I disturbed a roe deer. Next morning one walked past, probably the same one, I was upwind of it and although I was sitting still I think it had a good idea I was there. But it just ambled on.

You can tell attitudes are changing; the chewing gum papers littered along this track now have 'Keep your country tidy!' printed on them.

A forestry tractor and trailer rattling by must have put up blow-flies basking on the sand. I couldn't easily write with thirty or forty of them humming about me so I took the opportunity to look for the once-smelt-never-to-be-forgotten stinkhorns I had been getting whiffs of.

ANTS POURED OUT HERE WHEN I LAY DOWN TO DRAW. AND THERE WERE DOZENS OF SPIDERS AND HARVESTMEN ON THIS SMALL PATCH OF GROUND.

I didn't have to look far to find the stinkhorns, there were half a dozen within two yards. The scent is supposed to attract blow-flies which then spread the spores. An enterprising spider had spun its web right over the remains of one stinkhorn.

35

SLIGHTLY ALARMED
& NEUROTIC
Chic chic   Chic-chic Chic chic

WHEN ONE
SAW ME HARSHER
Chi-arrgh

Glaucous
bulrush

Martham Broad *July*

There is a tern colony here on the
Norfolk Naturalists' Trust reserve.
The terns keep emerging from the reedbeds and flying a straight line into the
wind, a slow fluttery flight, dipping
sporadically. But the wind has built up
now, the water has become choppy
and I can see only one bird, fishing
along the far side of the broad in
the shelter of a reed-bed.

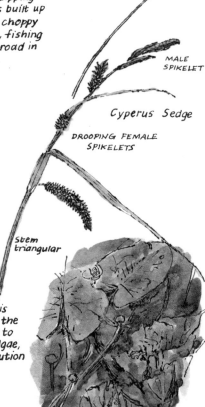

MALE
SPIKELET

Cyperus Sedge

DROOPING FEMALE
SPIKELETS

Stem
triangular

Alder

The froth that is
blown up against the
shore here is due to
the activity of algae,
I believe, not pollution
by detergents.

The submerged leaves of yellow
water-lily look like crumpled
rhubarb or lettuce.

Horsetail
Stem

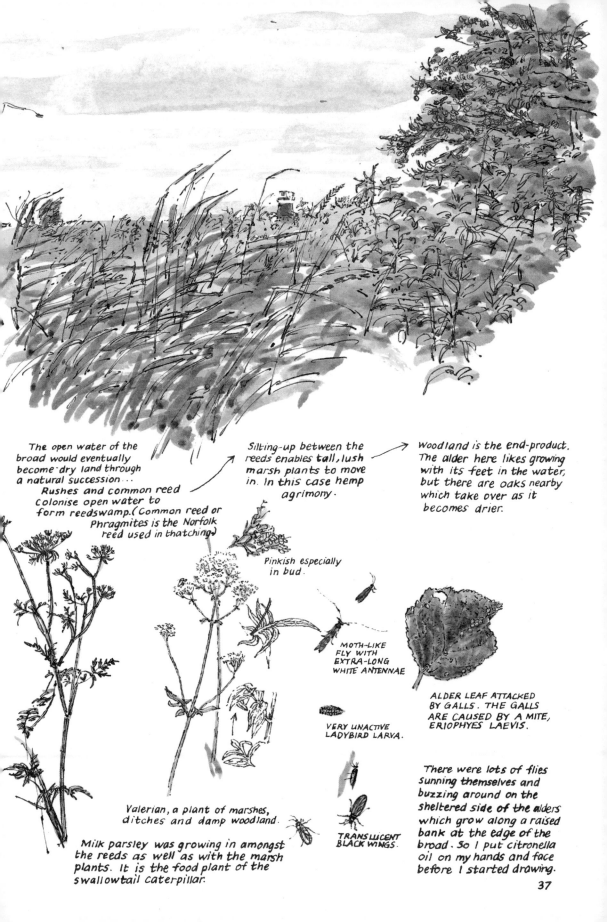

The open water of the broad would eventually become dry land through a natural succession...

Rushes and common reed colonise open water to form reedswamp. (Common reed or Phragmites is the Norfolk reed used in thatching.)

Silting-up between the reeds enables tall, lush marsh plants to move in. In this case hemp agrimony.

Woodland is the end-product. The alder here likes growing with its feet in the water, but there are oaks nearby which take over as it becomes drier.

Pinkish especially in bud.

MOTH-LIKE FLY WITH EXTRA-LONG WHITE ANTENNAE

VERY UNACTIVE LADYBIRD LARVA.

ALDER LEAF ATTACKED BY GALLS. THE GALLS ARE CAUSED BY A MITE, ERIOPHYES LAEVIS.

Valerian, a plant of marshes, ditches and damp woodland.

Milk parsley was growing in amongst the reeds as well as with the marsh plants. It is the food plant of the swallowtail caterpillar.

TRANSLUCENT BLACK WINGS.

There were lots of flies sunning themselves and buzzing around on the sheltered side of the alders which grow along a raised bank at the edge of the broad. So I put citronella oil on my hands and face before I started drawing.

37

Cley next the Sea
Norfolk July

From a hide on the Norfolk Naturalists' Trust Reserve

← Feet show

KEE HAR! YAR!

Heron mobbed by black-headed gulls.

Plenty of avocets about, I can count something like eleven out there at the moment (they keep waltzing behind islands or changing into shelduck in the distance).

suwi! swui!

Confrontation between 3 or 4 avocets and a number of mallard ducks who have now settled down to rest in the grass.

Bearded tit (minus beard... and come to think of it, it isn't even a tit. Better called a reedling).

SIMILAR PATTERN OF ROTORS TO THE WINDMILL AT CLEY.

Black-tailed godwits, long straight bill and long legs. And they have a handsomely marked underwing.

IT DIDN'T HAVE MUCH OF A TAIL.

Black-headed gull drinking.

These sedge warblers are just that bit smaller than I expected them to be; bigger than a wren but a good deal smaller than a sparrow.

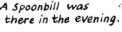

A Spoonbill was there in the evening.

One moorhen chased another over the shallow water until it turned head down, wings ruffled out and tail up. I've come to expect this kind of aggression from moorhens, what I didn't expect was the gentleness when the one that had been chased and its mate groomed each other. The one being groomed stood motionless, its head bent in a balletic gesture.

A tangle of fool's watercress growing on wet ground by the railway sleeper path.

Wild celery, the leaves do have a strong smell of celery when crushed.

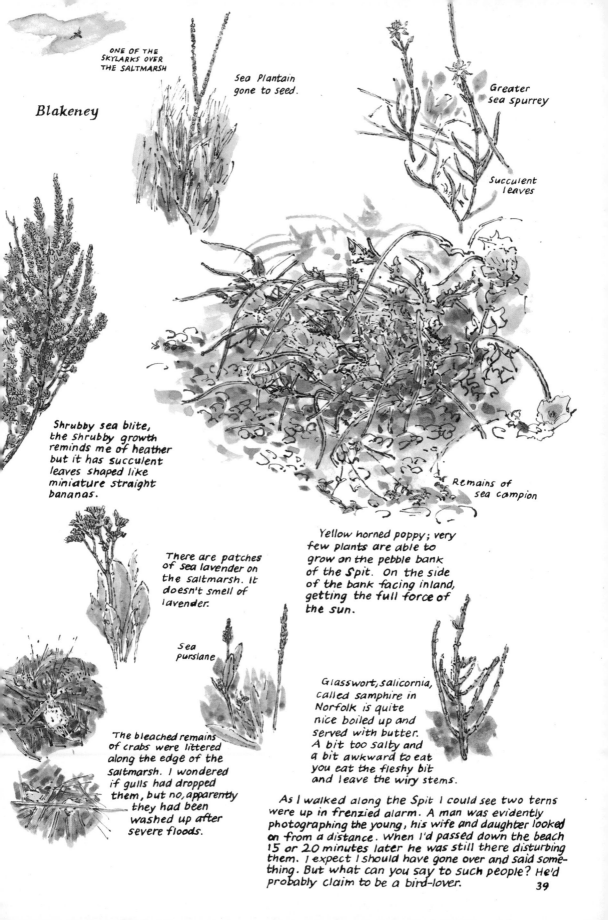

ONE OF THE
SKYLARKS OVER
THE SALTMARSH

Sea Plantain
gone to seed.

Greater
sea spurrey

Succulent
leaves

Blakeney

Shrubby sea blite,
the shrubby growth
reminds me of heather
but it has succulent
leaves shaped like
miniature straight
bananas.

Remains of
sea campion

There are patches
of sea lavender on
the saltmarsh. It
doesn't smell of
lavender.

Yellow horned poppy; very
few plants are able to
grow on the pebble bank
of the Spit. On the side
of the bank facing inland,
getting the full force of
the sun.

Sea
purslane

Glasswort, salicornia,
called samphire in
Norfolk is quite
nice boiled up and
served with butter.
A bit too salty and
a bit awkward to eat
you eat the fleshy bit
and leave the wiry stems.

The bleached remains
of crabs were littered
along the edge of the
saltmarsh. I wondered
if gulls had dropped
them, but no, apparently
they had been
washed up after
severe floods.

As I walked along the Spit I could see two terns
were up in frenzied alarm. A man was evidently
photographing the young, his wife and daughter looked
on from a distance. When I'd passed down the beach
15 or 20 minutes later he was still there disturbing
them. I expect I should have gone over and said something. But what can you say to such people? He'd
probably claim to be a bird-lover.

39

Poplars at Eye   Suffolk, July

Today is so still that even these poplars are not trembling and shimmering. But they still remind me of an Impressionist painting. Each leaf is a different modulation of colour... blue greens, yellow greens.

I CAN HEAR AN EXOTIC BIRD CALL WHICH SOUNDS LIKE A SQUEAKY ROUNDABOUT. IN FACT IT PROBABLY IS A SQUEAKY ROUNDABOUT— THERE CAN'T BE MANY SOUTH AMERICAN BELL- BIRDS ROUND HERE.

THERE IS A CONTINUOUS BUZZING IN THE POPLAR ABOVE MY HEAD. MAINLY OF HOVERFLIES.

Scerunch
Scerunch

My train of thought about painting was interupted by the sound of grass tearing. A patch of the ground a yard or two from me was moving up and down. A few minutes later the movement started again, closer to me. A mole perhaps? There are mole-hills on the playing field nearby. The movement had that kind of power.

Just brushing my hair made 34 of these minute insects fall onto the page. There must be two hundred on my shirt and arms. They resemble very small Devil's coach horses. I think they are thrips (and therefore not related to the Devil's coach horse). They're called thunder flies because they take wing in large numbers on still summer days.

Black poplar; probably these trees are a fast- growing hybrid of black poplar.

When I walk along the path this young thrush hops along in front of me.

40

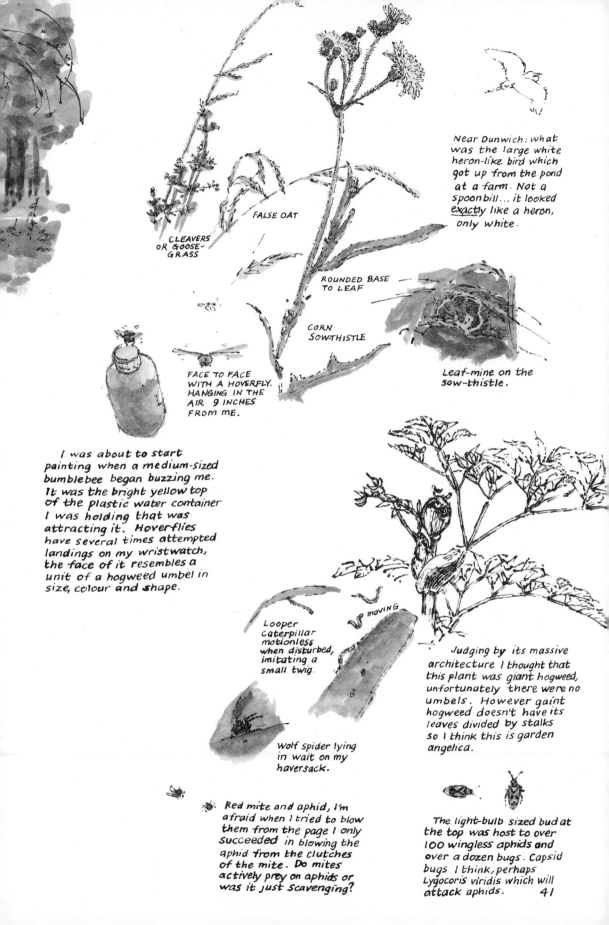

CLEAVERS OR GOOSE-GRASS

FALSE OAT

ROUNDED BASE TO LEAF

CORN SOW-THISTLE

Near Dunwich: what was the large white heron-like bird which got up from the pond at a farm. Not a spoonbill... it looked <u>exactly</u> like a heron, only white.

Leaf-mine on the sow-thistle.

FACE TO FACE WITH A HOVERFLY. HANGING IN THE AIR 9 INCHES FROM ME.

I was about to start painting when a medium-sized bumblebee began buzzing me. It was the bright yellow top of the plastic water container I was holding that was attracting it. Hoverflies have several times attempted landings on my wristwatch, the face of it resembles a unit of a hogweed umbel in size, colour and shape.

Looper caterpillar motionless when disturbed, imitating a small twig.

MOVING

Wolf spider lying in wait on my haversack.

Judging by its massive architecture I thought that this plant was giant hogweed, unfortunately there were no umbels. However gaint hogweed doesn't have its leaves divided by stalks so I think this is garden angelica.

Red mite and aphid, I'm afraid when I tried to blow them from the page I only succeeded in blowing the aphid from the clutches of the mite. Do mites actively prey on aphids or was it just scavenging?

The light-bulb sized bud at the top was host to over 100 wingless aphids and over a dozen bugs. Capsid bugs I think, perhaps Lygocoris viridis which will attack aphids. 41

Surface of
water entirely
covered with
duckweed. So that
flies can walk about.

42

Landed on
page &
turned its head
about looking aroun

A Ditch in Dedham Vale
Suffolk
July

It would have been superfluous to have drawn the general landscape, the vale so accurately resembled Constable's paintings, especially at this time of the year with heavy summer greenness and ripening corn. The straw is gathered in giant swiss rolls instead of sheaves, but they catch the sunlight just as effectively.

I called at Flatford Mill, now a Field Study Centre, to borrow a pond net and a pie dish so that I could find out what pond life there was in the ditch.

A small colony of marsh woundwort was growing out of the water in the bottom of the ditch.

Small water beetles clambering among weeds.

The young of a pond skater, it has no wings as yet. With all that duckweed there is no room to skate. This one made hops across the surface when I released it.

Mite adrift on pad of duckweed

Transparent discarded skin of a mosquito larva. Either shed when it grew or became a pupa, or perhaps this ghostly shell is all that is left after a predatory insect sucked its soft body out.

water starwort

Reddish, expanding and contracting, transparent with zig-zag gut showing. I should have brought a hand lens.

This diving beetle reminded me of an almond. Smaller than the margined Dytiscus water beetle, it was built on the same pattern. Underneath shaped like a shallow draughted boat. I reckon it was a Colymbetes beetle (C. fuscus?)

Also present: those tiny creatures that swim by bending into figure of eight shapes.

A microscope would have revealed a great deal more in the pond. I could just make out the rabbit's head shape of Cyclops – a body with a single eye and trailing egg-sacs.

Four sticklebacks from one sweep of the net, must be a large number in the ditch; the three-spined variety.

Like a small version of the great pond snail, probably the marsh snail, Lymnaea palustris.

SILVER LINE OF AIR BUBBLE TRAPPED ON BRISTLY HAIRS OF ABDOMEN.

I keep netting black slimy mud from the bottom of the ditch. The blood-worm has haemoglobin in its body in order to store oxygen to enable it to survive in these oxygen poor conditions.

An odd-looking 'fly' landed on the page, one of the water boatmen in the pie dish had taken off. But its legs aren't designed for use on land and it slid off the page onto my anorak. I shook it back into the water.

All the boatmen I caught swam right way up so they were all lesser waterboatmen, Corixa. The other sort of water-boatman is Notonecta, the backswimmer.

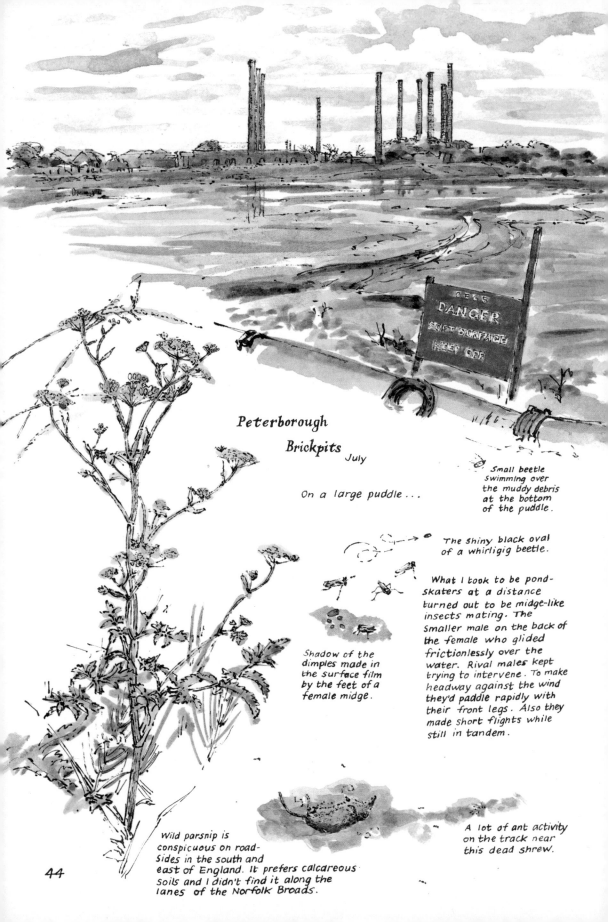

DANGER
SOFT SURFACE
KEEP OFF

Peterborough

Brickpits July

On a large puddle...

Small beetle swimming over the muddy debris at the bottom of the puddle.

The shiny black oval of a whirligig beetle.

What I took to be pond-skaters at a distance turned out to be midge-like insects mating. The smaller male on the back of the female who glided frictionlessly over the water. Rival males kept trying to intervene. To make headway against the wind they'd paddle rapidly with their front legs. Also they made short flights while still in tandem.

Shadow of the dimples made in the surface film by the feet of a female midge.

A lot of ant activity on the track near this dead shrew.

Wild parsnip is conspicuous on road-sides in the south and east of England. It prefers calcareous soils and I didn't find it along the lanes of the Norfolk Broads.

My landlady told me about the brickpits;
"When they're left the holes sometimes fill with
water; always fish will appear and often it'll be
pike, big pike. Nobody puts them there, they form
themselves like woodworm form in wood. Mice
do that as well, they'll form themselves where
there've been none before."

The brickpits appealed to me as an extreme example
of industrial activity changing the landscape, a
contrast to the natural richness of East Anglia.
But the derelict brickyards were rich in wildlife, in
fact there was more of interest here than in the
huge fields of open fenland farms. Plants of rough
ground and marshy ground had moved in on the
old brickfield, there were insects in abundance;
electric-blue damselflies, bumble-bees busy pollinating
flowers. Skylarks and a yellowhammer singing.
Partridge on rough ground, a pied wagtail
hunting over a railway track.
Sparrows were nesting in the
wooden vents of one building.

Melilot, ribbed melilot I guess,
a plant of waste places
introduced from Europe.

Gulls roosted
on the mud
slurry of
the fly-ash
lagoons.

Nibbled grass.
I can hear grass-
hoppers, a small
one with only
one back
leg jumped
onto the
page.

About two-thirds the
size of a tortoiseshell,
stopping briefly on
lesser bindweed...
a gatekeeper female,
typical of lowland
England.

An extensive bricked-
over area gives an
opportunity for
an extensive
and roomy
rabbit warren.

RABBIT
PELLETS

← SILK EGG-COCOON

I don't think
this wolf spider
could see where
she was going, her head-end
was covered with a dozen or
more young and she was
still carrying
the egg-
cocoon.

PORCUPINE-BOMB SEEDS

Wild carrot, the umbels
close up tightly when they
go to seed, in this case
trapping bleached seed
heads of cocksfoot grass.

As the prickly seeds
develop the head opens
out again.

Centipede-rapid
sinuous run for
cover.

MUGWORT

Earwig holding its
pincers scorpion-fashion.

Beneath a brick
it had a sort
of burrow- with
a small chamber
it was apparently
digging at the
far end away
from the entrance.

SCURRYING
GROUND BEETLE

"Are you a train-spotter?"
"No, I'm drawing rabbit holes."
"I didn't think you were but
then I saw that you started
writing whenever a train came
past."
"Well, I feel so exposed here; everytime
an Intercity 125 comes past I feel there
are 300 people watching me and I'd
better do some work!"

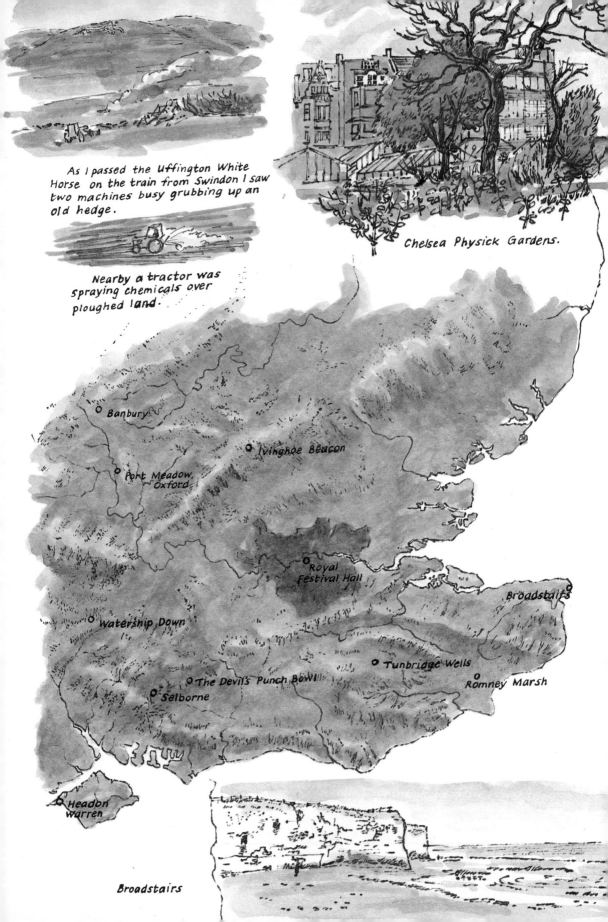

As I passed the Uffington White Horse on the train from Swindon I saw two machines busy grubbing up an old hedge.

Nearby a tractor was spraying chemicals over ploughed land.

Chelsea Physick Gardens.

Banbury

Ivinghoe Beacon

Port Meadow, Oxford

Royal Festival Hall

Broadstairs

Watership Down

Tunbridge Wells

The Devil's Punch Bowl

Romney Marsh

Selborne

Headon Warren

Broadstairs

DOWNLANDS AND THE WEALD

August–October

Living in the north it is easy to get the impression that south of Stevenage England is more or less built up, with a few sad fields, riding stables and boarding kennels to punctuate interminable housing estates. With its many towns and long history of farming, I thought the countryside in the south would seem man-made, not at all wild. But I had underestimated both its wildness and its variety. There are quiet beechwoods and rough commons with golden yellow gorse and slender birches. In parts of the Weald there is thick, impenetrable woodland, and one heather-covered clearing among Scots pines on a hillside bore an uncanny resemblance to parts of Scotland that I know. Along the coast there is undisturbed marshland and long stretches of deserted cliff top. From the lonely windswept summits of the Downs there are wide panoramas of patchwork fields stretching into the distance.

I remember my first visit to Box Hill, one of the highest parts of Surrey. I was impressed by how many miles I could walk without coming to a road; in fact I managed to get lost as I explored. The steep slopes are clothed in dense woodland and besides oak, ash and beech there is yew, wild cherry, whitebeam and box – trees which are rare or absent in the northern woods I'm familiar with. Unfortunately, however, it is not always as unspoilt as this. The hills and woods around the village of Cookham look as inviting to walk in as they do in Stanley Spencer's paintings, but before I'd got far I was turned back by 'Keep Out' notices, high wire fences and warnings about guard dog patrols. Not very welcoming. It is certainly worth having an Ordnance Survey map to enable you to find public footpaths.

I stayed in youth hostels on this trip when I wasn't staying with friends. The ones in the south are variable. A superior hostel on the Isle of Wight had the air of a private hotel while the most primitive, an ancient cottage deep in the Devil's Punch Bowl, had a wood fire and a tap but no electricity. I didn't think there would be places as wild and remote as this in the south of England. I was only a few miles from the streets and houses of Guildford. Yet here, in this utterly secluded valley, its slopes thick with bracken and brambles, trees, fungi and wild plants, I could have been a hundred miles from the nearest town.

The hostel at Ivinghoe had a particularly happy atmosphere and I quickly felt at home. The village itself is quite small, with a wooden windmill and a cross-shaped church with a tower in the middle, and is completely dominated by Ivinghoe Beacon which rises dramatically above the surrounding countryside. This is a popular spot, because it is where walkers who start the Ridgeway at Avebury finish their journey and exchange tales of their adventures. But the country all round Ivinghoe, where there are ancient beechwoods and magnificent views across the Chiltern Hills, is well worth a visit on its own account.

The Ridgeway itself follows the high open tops of the chalk downs. Originally it must have provided a relatively quick and direct route across England to the West Country, for by sticking to the tops of the hills the traveller could avoid the thick forest and marshland that made travel difficult, and dangerous, on lower ground. The antiquity of the Ridgeway can be judged by the number of pre-Roman sites along its 85-mile length, from the stone circle at Avebury to the Iron Age hill fort at Ivinghoe Beacon. But the Uffington horse, near Swindon, was probably cut in the turf after the Romans had left Britain. Rabbits and sheep have kept the grassy upland clear of trees and on the lower ground the woods have all but disappeared. As I passed the White Horse on the train from Swindon I saw two machines busy grubbing up an old hedge, while near by a tractor was spraying chemicals over ploughed land.

My visit to another part of southern England began rather hectically – I arrived in Broadstairs at the start of a Bank Holiday weekend. The town was far more crowded than I had anticipated, with cars and people pouring in from all directions. I had considerable trouble finding some-where to stay. It may seem strange to expect to find wildlife in a busy seaside town, but even a crowded holiday beach has an abundance of marine animals and plants in rock pools and along the shoreline. And there were birds and lichens and more plants along the cliff tops. It was much the same on Romney Marsh, with the Cinque Ports and the coast attracting many visitors. But inland the marsh levels are still lonely places where wildlife can flourish undisturbed, although the Royal Military Canal attracts a lot of anglers.

Perhaps I was most surprised by the wild quality of the Weald. I hadn't expected to find such a rugged landscape in this part of the country. Alternating layers of harder free-draining sand and softer impervious clays give a dramatically varied effect. The domed structure makes the Weald a likely place to find oil, which is why gargantuan survey vehicles had invaded the narrow lanes near Tunbridge Wells when I was there in

September. At one time the whole of the Weald must have been capped by chalk but, weakened by folding, this has been eroded away until a rim around the edge is all that remains – the North and South Downs.

The whale-backed downs of southern England are graceful rather than rugged. Somehow the gently flowing lines of downland seem to be reflected in the elegant plots of Jane Austen's novels. Many novelists have an intuitive appreciation of landscape and their characters move convincingly in a setting they belong to and from which they grow. Dickens does not immediately strike one as a regional author, but his speciality was to catch the flavour of life in the London Basin; the Thames and its estuary figure large in his work. Certain of his characters are irrevocably associated with a particular location – young Pip on the Romney Marshes or David Copperfield's aunt, Betsy Trotwood, in her house on the chalk cliffs at Broadstairs.

The countryside farther to the west is also full of associations for me, particularly Selborne where I stayed at the old inn just across the road from Gilbert White's house, The Wakes. Visiting the house in late afternoon it wasn't hard to picture the isolated village as it must have been 200 years ago. Across the lawn you can follow the same stone path that White used. It leads to a reconstruction of the wooden shelter he built as a hide for watching birds. Beyond the fields at the end of the garden the steep chalk scarp rises and The Zigzag path climbs through a beechwood.

When I was in Southampton after visiting Selborne I picked up a paper-back of D. H. Lawrence short stories which included *The Man Who Loved Islands*. It was a strange coincidence that I should be reading this while waiting for the ferry to the Isle of Wight. Islands do have a unique quality. The man in the story loved them so much that he moved to ever smaller islands . . . just as I was planning to move on to Skokholm in the springtime.

Made off very slowly
flying amongst the willows.

Willows near Banbury

August

A grey squirrel moving
through the trees
reminded me of film I've
seen of colobus monkeys
making their way from
tree to tree in the
forest canopy.

Something was tearing
at grass stems and moving
the buttercup leaves nearby.
A water vole? No it must
have been something
smaller or I should have
seen it there.

A bright yellow
ex-GPO telephone van
acted as a super-
stimulus to 60
or 70 hoverflies.

In the morning, as the
sun began to get through,
each umbel of flowers
was studded with about
30 flies, mainly hoverflies.

A wasp had developed an ambush technique;
it kept flying up beneath umbels then pouncing
on unsuspecting insects that were feeding on top.
Soon it had attacked insects on all the nearby
umbels without catching any.

The cushion galls on these
leaves were made by Pontania
sawflies.

Green shoots springing from a
willow log: crack willows often
spread in this way when branches
break off a tree and sprout
new leaves and roots.

50

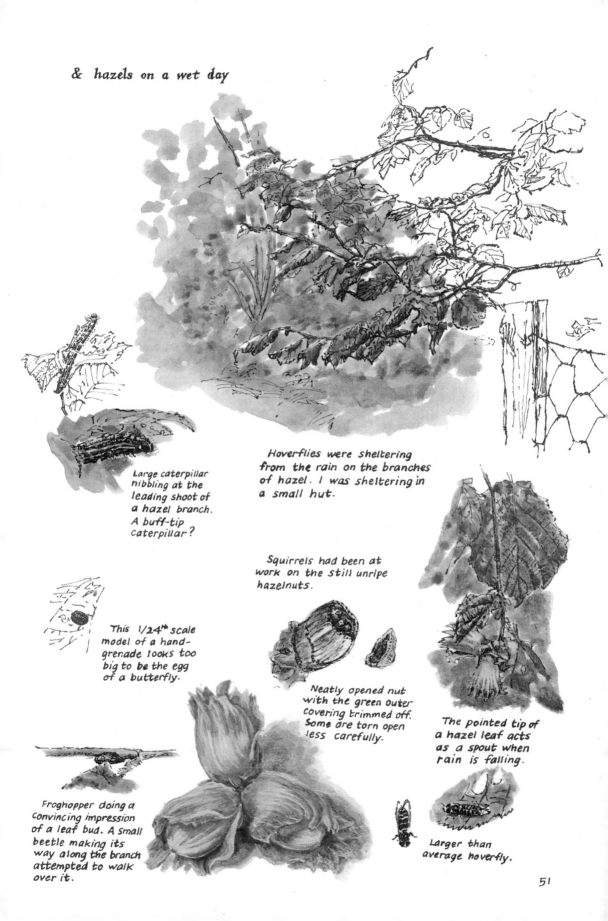

& hazels on a wet day

Large caterpillar nibbling at the leading shoot of a hazel branch. A buff-tip caterpillar?

Hoverflies were sheltering from the rain on the branches of hazel. I was sheltering in a small hut.

Squirrels had been at work on the still unripe hazelnuts.

This 1/24th scale model of a hand-grenade looks too big to be the egg of a butterfly.

Neatly opened nut with the green outer covering trimmed off. Some are torn open less carefully.

The pointed tip of a hazel leaf acts as a spout when rain is falling.

Froghopper doing a convincing impression of a leaf bud. A small beetle making its way along the branch attempted to walk over it.

Larger than average hoverfly.

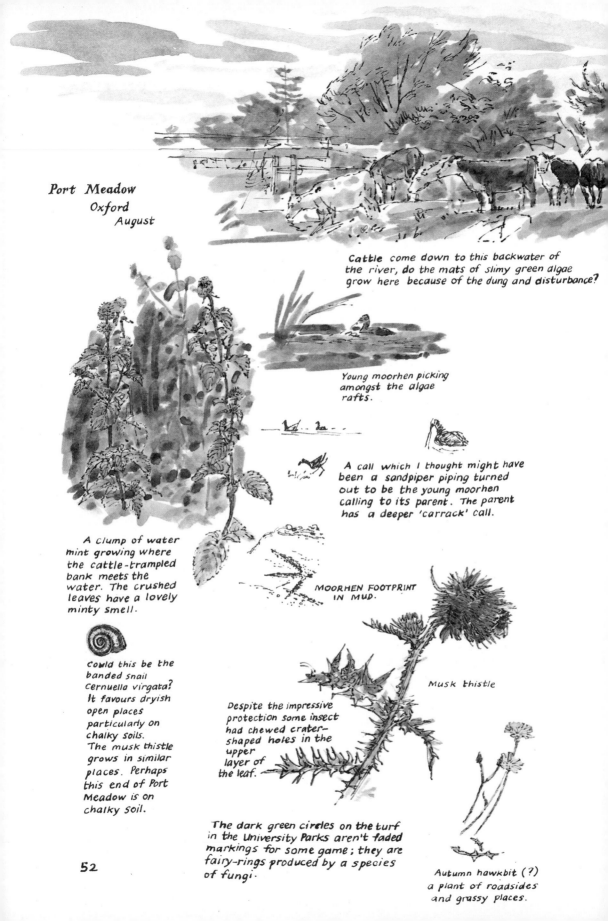

Port Meadow
Oxford
August

Cattle come down to this backwater of the river, do the mats of slimy green algae grow here because of the dung and disturbance?

Young moorhen picking amongst the algae rafts.

A call which I thought might have been a sandpiper piping turned out to be the young moorhen calling to its parent. The parent has a deeper 'carrack' call.

A clump of water mint growing where the cattle-trampled bank meets the water. The crushed leaves have a lovely minty smell.

MOORHEN FOOTPRINT IN MUD.

Could this be the banded snail Cernuella virgata? It favours dryish open places particularly on chalky soils. The musk thistle grows in similar places. Perhaps this end of Port Meadow is on chalky soil.

Musk thistle

Despite the impressive protection some insect had chewed crater-shaped holes in the upper layer of the leaf.

The dark green circles on the turf in the University Parks aren't faded markings for some game; they are fairy-rings produced by a species of fungi.

Autumn hawkbit (?) a plant of roadsides and grassy places.

52

A charm of nine jingling goldfinches
went by, they have a slender beak
by comparison with other finches and
are acrobatic, so getting at the seeds
in the downy heads of thistle is
one of their specialities.

Creeping thistle

Seven-spot
ladybird

53

GREY
SQUIRREL

Beech Hanger
near Ivinghoe Beacon
The Chilterns
August

While I was in the woods a thunderstorm started. As I hurried back through the fields I saw the lofty chimneys of the cement works struck by lightning several times.
I was glad not to be the tallest object in the landscape.

My thermos flask attracted an audience of 18 hoverflies.

Common helleborine, an orchid of shady places, grows up to 2 feet tall.

On the path through the fields to the beech wood I found this peacock butterfly, its outer wings black and slightly iridescent.

As I drew it sat trembling. Then it opened its wings to show the stunning pattern inside and flapped off noisily.

LARGE HEAP OF EXCAVATED MATERIAL INCLUDES CHALK BOULDERS UP TO 4" ACROSS.

PATH

PATH

PATH

Looks like Clavaria corniculata, one of the 'fairy clubs', except that grows in grass, this was on well rotted wood.

54

Following a well-worn path I was surprised when the overhanging branches got lower and lower, until they were only 2 or 3 feet above the path. Halfway up the hillside I found a large burrow, the entrance to a badger sett – what else could dig out all that rubble?
Three paths led off through the dense woodland.

Jackdaw calls exploding, nasal songs of tits in the tree canopy, the clatter of a wood pigeon, a wren scolding, basset hounds barking, a passenger jet overhead... When I lived in London the London Transport Country Walks book took me through acres of Chilterns beechwoods. So I remember heavy sticky mud, the earth dotted with flints, the smell of damp wood land, leaf litter and beechmast on the ground.

The leaf canopy of beech is so effective that the shrub layer and herb layer are often shaded out.

Bulgaria inquinans has a rubbery texture.

Bracket fungus sprouting from the stump of a fallen beech. Like a cumulus cloud modelled in dough, with banding which reminds me of the cloud belts of Jupiter.
Ganoderma applanatum... or Fomes?

Broadstairs
August

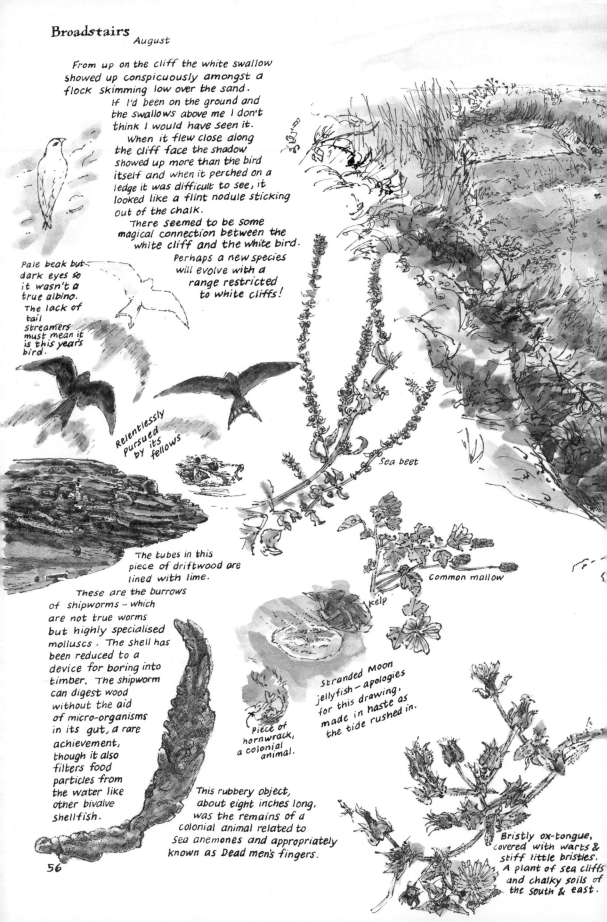

From up on the cliff the white swallow showed up conspicuously amongst a flock skimming low over the sand.

If I'd been on the ground and the swallows above me I don't think I would have seen it.

When it flew close along the cliff face the shadow showed up more than the bird itself and when it perched on a ledge it was difficult to see, it looked like a flint nodule sticking out of the chalk.

There seemed to be some magical connection between the white cliff and the white bird.

Perhaps a new species will evolve with a range restricted to white cliffs!

Pale beak but dark eyes so it wasn't a true albino.
The lack of tail streamers must mean it is this year's bird.

Relentlessly pursued by its fellows

Sea beet

The tubes in this piece of driftwood are lined with lime.

These are the burrows of shipworms – which are not true worms but highly specialised molluscs. The shell has been reduced to a device for boring into timber. The shipworm can digest wood without the aid of micro-organisms in its gut, a rare achievement, though it also filters food particles from the water like other bivalve shellfish.

Common mallow

Kelp

Piece of hornwrack, a colonial animal.

Stranded Moon jellyfish – apologies for this drawing, made in haste as the tide rushed in.

This rubbery object, about eight inches long, was the remains of a colonial animal related to sea anemones and appropriately known as Dead men's fingers.

Bristly ox-tongue, covered with warts & stiff little bristles. A plant of sea cliffs and chalky soils of the south & east.

56

WRONG!

NEARER

Rescue helicopters **are** surprisingly difficult to draw, they bulge out where you don't **expect** them to.

Sea rocket, on the sand at the foot of the cliff.

Globular seed capsule

seeds

Sea purslane, Honkenya peploides, was spreading over the dry sand at the top of the beach. It had bright green fleshy leaves, like the succulent plants of deserts.

SMALL POOL ON THE BEACH

Chalk

Lugworm casts

Kelp

holdfast

Edible crab (deceased)

Delta where water flows into the pool.

This ferocious flexible bodied creature bit the boy who tried to pick it up for me. It was a Devil's coach horse...I had a feeling it might bite – that's why I let him pick it up! Quite a few were wandering over the cliff and sand below.

The camouflage of this goby exactly matched the sand. Would a different coloured beach have different coloured gobies? They cast no shadow when at rest and I only noticed them when they darted towards the dead crab which I'd put in the pool in the hope it might revive.

57

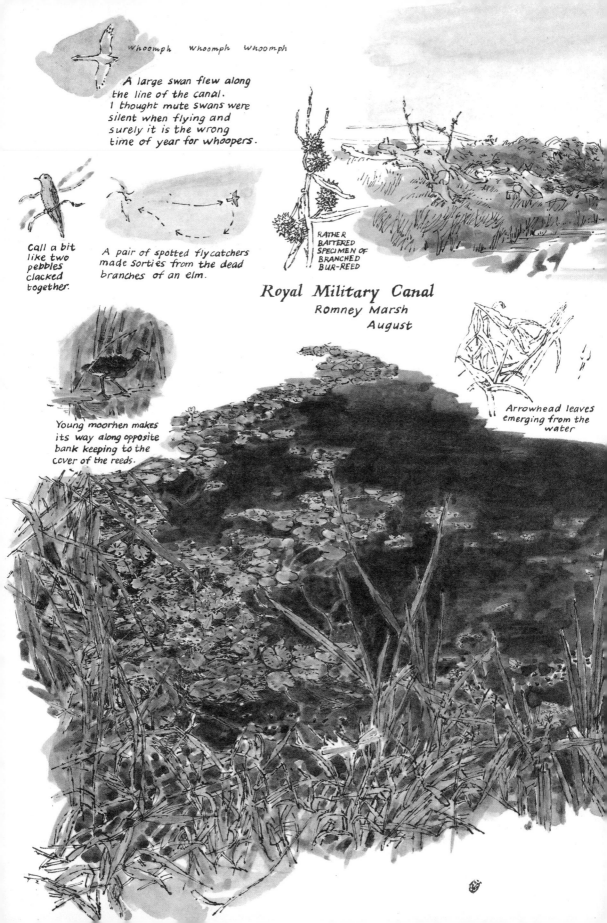

whoomph   whoomph   whoomph

A large swan flew along
the line of the canal.
I thought mute swans were
silent when flying and
surely it is the wrong
time of year for whoopers.

Call a bit
like two
pebbles
clacked
together.

A pair of spotted flycatchers
made sorties from the dead
branches of an elm.

RATHER
BATTERED
SPECIMEN OF
BRANCHED
BUR-REED

Royal Military Canal
Romney Marsh
August

Young moorhen makes
its way along opposite
bank keeping to the
cover of the reeds.

Arrowhead leaves
emerging from the
water

GREAT
WATER PLANTAIN

CODLINS
& CREAM

PHRAGMITES-
COMMON REED

Sheep here are marked
with a bright blue
anchor. The Blue Anchor
is a local
pub.

I spent a long time sitting by the canal
on my collapsible stool drawing the
yellow water-lilies and bankside vegetation.
"Have you caught anything?" two lads
asked me. They'd caught 5 roaches.
They seem very **knowledgeable**, these
young anglers; utterly involved in
what they are doing in a way which
is quite rare. And keenly observant:
"That wasn't a roach," I heard one
lad saying, "a roach has 3 orange fins."

I returned to the canal at twilight.
The sky was clear but a sparse pearly
mist breathed from the flat fields of
the marsh. A waning half-moon hung
on the power lines, the reflection of the
pole was broken into a changing sequence
of parallelograms by a fish rising.
There was a delicious chill in the air. An
owl was calling over the stubble fields.
The one called from the branches of
the dying elm above me. The dark
branches gave a stark wintry effect
on a summer's evening, they seemed
rooted in the stars. Bats were flying.

The black oval blobs are whirligig beetles
which live on the surface film of the water.
One caught a dead fly and a whirling slapstick
chase followed. At one stage three of the
pursuers chased each other in ever decreasing
circles while the one who actually had the fly
made off unmolested.

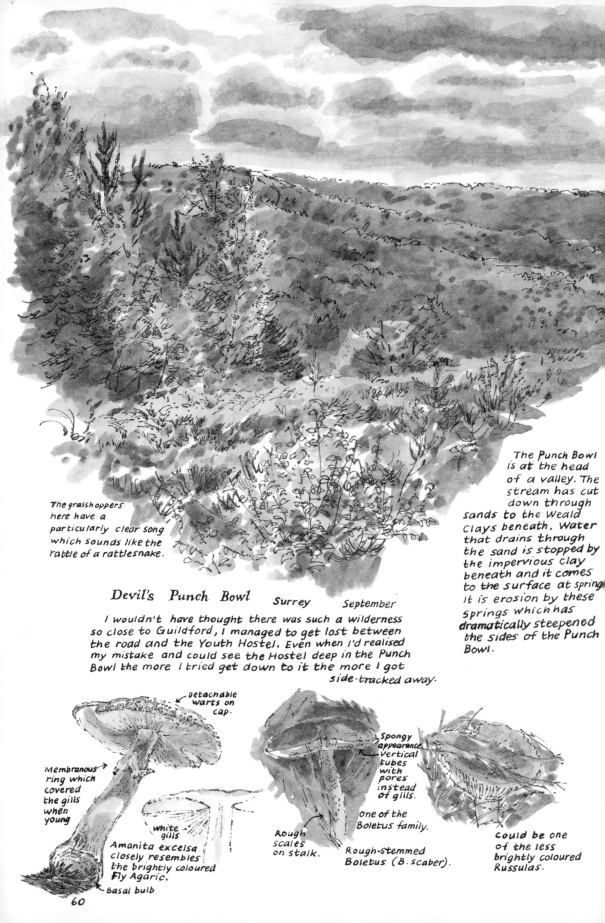

The grasshoppers here have a particularly clear song which sounds like the rattle of a rattlesnake.

The Punch Bowl is at the head of a valley. The stream has cut down through sands to the Weald Clays beneath. Water that drains through the sand is stopped by the impervious clay beneath and it comes to the surface at spring It is erosion by these springs which has **dramatically steepened** the sides of the Punch Bowl.

Devil's Punch Bowl Surrey September

I wouldn't have thought there was such a wilderness so close to Guildford, I managed to get lost between the road and the Youth Hostel. Even when I'd realised my mistake and could see the Hostel deep in the Punch Bowl the more I tried get down to it the more I got side-tracked away.

Detachable warts on cap.

Membranous ring which covered the gills when young

white gills

Amanita excelsa closely resembles the brightly coloured Fly Agaric.

Basal bulb

Spongy appearance Vertical tubes with pores instead of gills.

One of the Boletus family.

Rough scales on stalk.

Rough-stemmed Boletus (B. scaber).

Could be one of the less brightly coloured Russulas.

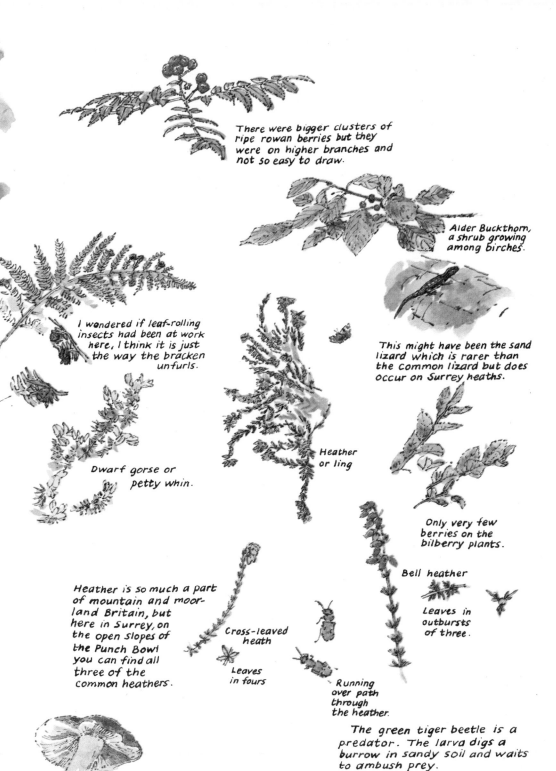

There were bigger clusters of ripe rowan berries but they were on higher branches and not so easy to draw.

Alder Buckthorn, a shrub growing among birches.

I wondered if leaf-rolling insects had been at work here, I think it is just the way the bracken unfurls.

This might have been the sand lizard which is rarer than the common lizard but does occur on Surrey heaths.

Dwarf gorse or petty whin.

Heather or ling

Only very few berries on the bilberry plants.

Bell heather

Leaves in outbursts of three.

Heather is so much a part of mountain and moorland Britain, but here in Surrey, on the open slopes of the Punch Bowl you can find all three of the common heathers.

Cross-leaved heath

Leaves in fours

Running over path through the heather.

The green tiger beetle is a predator. The larva digs a burrow in sandy soil and waits to ambush prey.

A typical Russula, this answers to the description of Russula emetica. But that grows near conifers... still, there was larch and pine nearby.

PERFECT HABITAT FOR SKATEBOARDERS

The Natural History of the Royal Festival Hall
London September

LAME SPARROW

Picking seeds from this tiny plant.

An odd coincidence; when I sat down in the café here and looked at the copy of today's Telegraph which had been left on the table I found an article about the South Bank by Alan Blyth. He described the very café I was in; the food is 'second to none in anonymity and dullness.'(Actually it was no worse than many other places!) And he described the approaches to the Festival Hall as 'an arid desert.'
Even a desert has some wildlife...

BLADDER FERN?

PIGEONS, USUALLY IN PAIRS.

In the entrance hall, polished slabs of limestone full of sea-lily fragments.

A busy ant colony behind a concrete block on the roof terrace.

Broad-leaved willowherb

Canadian Fleabane

SPORE CASE

SILVERY ENDS TO BRANCHES

This moss grew most luxuriantly along the eastern side of a sheltered walkway. The piece I drew was growing on a deposit of salts apparently dissolved out of the concrete.
Grimmia pulvinata, a common moss on walls.

Annual Meadow-grass

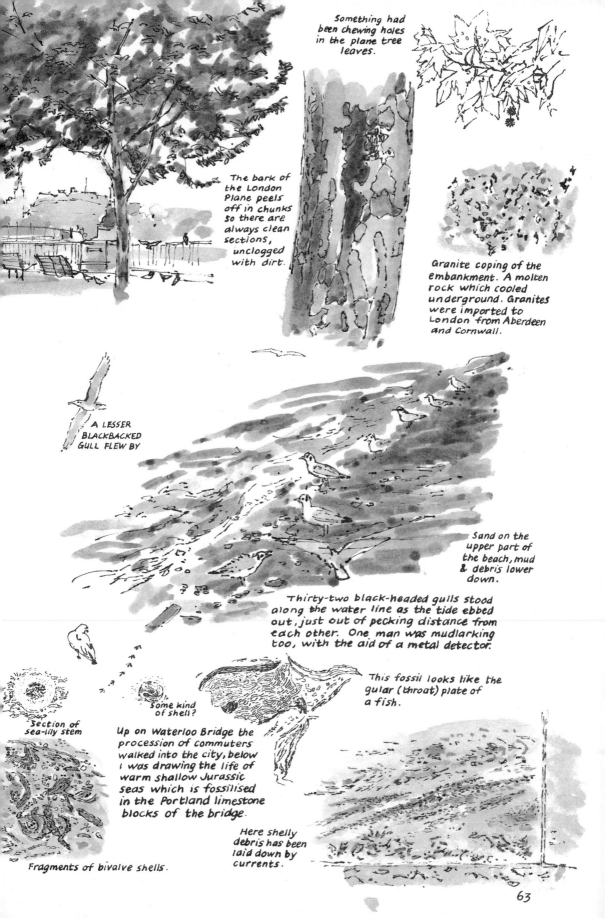

Something had been chewing holes in the plane tree leaves.

The bark of the London Plane peels off in chunks so there are always clean sections, unclogged with dirt.

Granite coping of the embankment. A molten rock which cooled underground. Granites were imported to London from Aberdeen and Cornwall.

A LESSER BLACKBACKED GULL FLEW BY

Sand on the upper part of the beach, mud & debris lower down.

Thirty-two black-headed gulls stood along the water line as the tide ebbed out, just out of pecking distance from each other. One man was mudlarking too, with the aid of a metal detector.

This fossil looks like the gular (throat) plate of a fish.

Section of sea-lily stem

Some kind of shell?

Up on Waterloo Bridge the procession of commuters walked into the city, below I was drawing the life of warm shallow Jurassic seas which is fossilised in the Portland limestone blocks of the bridge.

Here shelly debris has been laid down by currents.

Fragments of bivalve shells.

Return to Watership Down

Hampshire   September

Remains of an elm — I was sitting on the large sawn off stump, a favourite vantage point for pheasants to judge by the droppings and pheasants.

Richard Adams set his rabbit saga 'Watership Down' amongst the local fields, farms, hedges and ditches. There was a film version of the book, an animated cartoon, I did some work on the backgrounds specialising in close ups of hedgerows and rabbit holes. I wouldn't have missed out on the experience of working on the film for anything, the way it is made is fascinating. But it didn't really suit me; sitting in a studio in London trying to recreate in intimate rabbit's eye view detail this Berkshire/Hampshire landscape.

Returning to the real thing and climbing to the flat grassy expanse at the top of the down I found rows of plastic gorse bushes. They marked a course for race horse training.

Weasel ran across the field entrance

In a piece of chalk (coloured green by algae) there were fragments of shell. The chalk was laid down in clear seas which covered Britain some 70 million years ago.

woodlouse and centipede on underside of the piece of chalk.

Harebell

Small Scabious.

Fumitory?

Smooth Hawksbeard

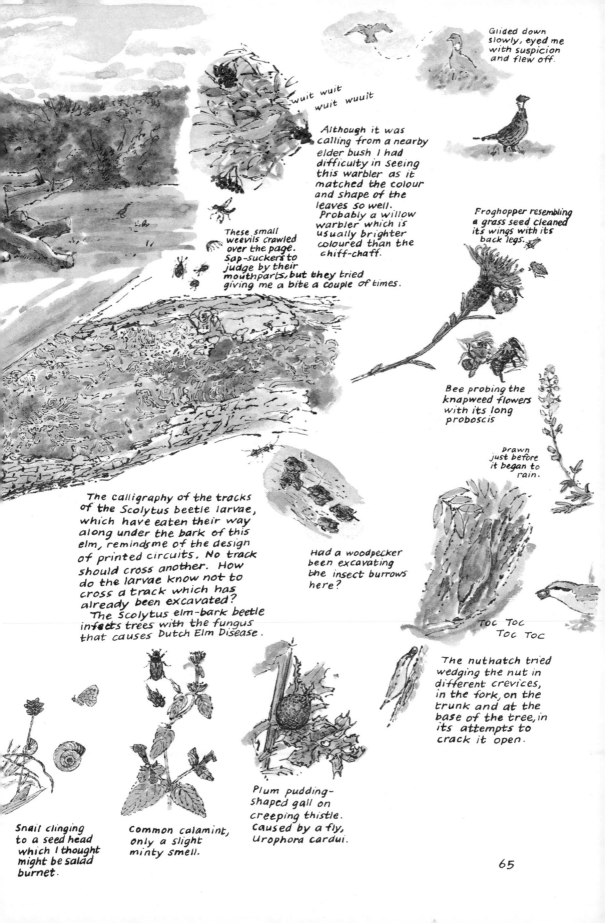

Glided down slowly, eyed me with suspicion and flew off.

wuit wuit wuit wuuit

Although it was calling from a nearby elder bush I had difficulty in seeing this warbler as it matched the colour and shape of the leaves so well. Probably a willow warbler which is usually brighter coloured than the chiff-chaff.

These small weevils crawled over the page. Sap-suckers to judge by their mouthparts, but they tried giving me a bite a couple of times.

Froghopper resembling a grass seed cleaned its wings with its back legs.

Bee probing the knapweed flowers with its long proboscis

Drawn just before it began to rain.

The calligraphy of the tracks of the Scolytus beetle larvae, which have eaten their way along under the bark of this elm, reminds me of the design of printed circuits. No track should cross another. How do the larvae know not to cross a track which has already been excavated?
The Scolytus elm-bark beetle infects trees with the fungus that causes Dutch Elm Disease.

Had a woodpecker been excavating the insect burrows here?

Toc Toc
Toc Toc

The nuthatch tried wedging the nut in different crevices, in the fork, on the trunk and at the base of the tree, in its attempts to crack it open.

Snail clinging to a seed head which I thought might be salad burnet.

Common calamint, only a slight minty smell.

Plum pudding-shaped gall on creeping thistle. Caused by a fly, Urophora cardui.

65

cho cho cho cho

Karr karrrh

The grey squirrel was
swearing vigorously at a
young mottled black cat.
The squirrels jerking tail
was as eloquent as its
scolding voice.

Ty'op Ty'op Ty'op Ty'op Ty'op
    Geeyar Geeyar
It had just collected an acorn
and when it found me drawing
at the foot of the tree it swore
at me for a couple of minutes.
I answered it back and it scampered
back up the tree and went round the long way.

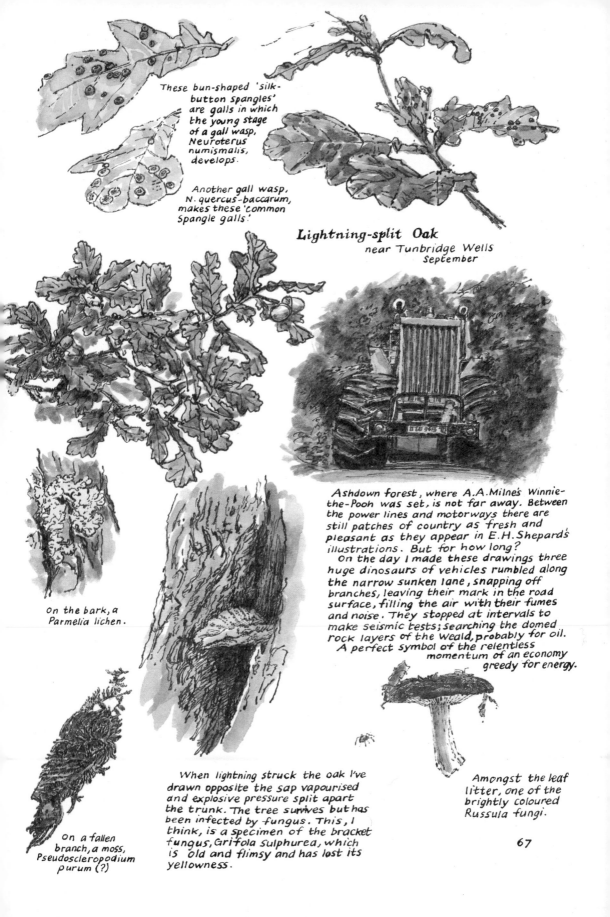

These bun-shaped 'silk-
button spangles'
are galls in which
the young stage
of a gall wasp,
Neuroterus
numismalis,
develops.

Another gall wasp,
N. quercus-baccarum,
makes these 'common
Spangle galls.'

Lightning-split Oak
near Tunbridge Wells
September

On the bark, a
Parmelia lichen.

Ashdown forest, where A.A.Milne's Winnie-
the-Pooh was set, is not far away. Between
the power lines and motorways there are
still patches of country as fresh and
pleasant as they appear in E.H.Shepard's
illustrations. But for how long?
    On the day I made these drawings three
huge dinosaurs of vehicles rumbled along
the narrow sunken lane, snapping off
branches, leaving their mark in the road
surface, filling the air with their fumes
and noise. They stopped at intervals to
make seismic tests; searching the domed
rock layers of the Weald, probably for oil.
    A perfect symbol of the relentless
                    momentum of an economy
                        greedy for energy.

On a fallen
branch, a moss,
Pseudoscleropodium
purum (?)

When lightning struck the oak I've
drawn opposite the sap vapourised
and explosive pressure split apart
the trunk. The tree survives but has
been infected by fungus. This, I
think, is a specimen of the bracket
fungus, Grifola sulphurea, which
is old and flimsy and has lost its
yellowness.

Amongst the leaf
litter, one of the
brightly coloured
Russula fungi.

67

This kestrel may have been a merlin, I'm told there was one near the Needles today. Flying fast over the cliff-top grassland.

Any amount of these beetles on the warren.

Day flying moth fluttering and investigating wood sage and honeysuckle. Probably a female, males generally have feathery antennae.

Yellow-wort, same family as the gentians. In the shelter of a bramble bush on the path to the Needles, on top of a chalk cliff. Note the way the rather fleshy leaves clasp the stem.

Betony suffering from exposure?

Autumn felwort. Many of these gentians had been eaten into, probably by the snails that abound here. Reasonably crushproof, on turf and chalk rubble by path.

Headon Warren

Isle of Wight   September

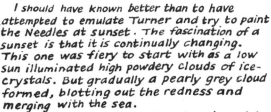

Very bushy tails

I should have known better than to have attempted to emulate Turner and try to paint the Needles at sunset. The fascination of a sunset is that it is continually changing. This one was fiery to start with as a low sun illuminated high powdery clouds of ice-crystals. But gradually a pearly grey cloud formed, blotting out the redness and merging with the sea.

Just as it was getting too dark to paint I heard calls in the pasture below the common which I thought might be owls. I saw a movement and with binoculars I could just make it out as a fox.

There were three of them. One ran at another that was sitting down and a tussle followed, then a chase. There was a noise of people along the lane, but the foxes appeared undisturbed and gradually made their way across the field, investigating as they went. And rolling! (I think).

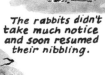

On the mainland I found only one colony of skate-boarders in an ideal habitat in the centre of London. They exist on this island in considerable numbers and have distinctively marked helmets and kneepads.

The rabbits didn't take much notice and soon resumed their nibbling.

This lends support to the observation that life-forms that have disappeared on the mainland survive on islands. E.G: The Lemurs of Madagascar.

¾ Life size. As it went marching over the path it was difficult to sort out the striking but disruptive pattern. So when it stopped to eat a sorrel leaf on the short rabbit-cropped turf I drew this detail.

Both look like caterpillars of the Fox moth, which lives on heath and moorland. As it grows the markings on the cater-pillar change.

A further caterpillar, not so big as the first and without the grey badger-like hair.

A horse shoe hole in the thin turf exposed the sand beneath. Fresh sand excavated from eight small holes showed conspicuously. I sat and drank my flask of coffee and watched to see if the occupants would appear. A small black head with neat yellow markings peered out. And a rear end, like a hoverfly but rounder, appeared, trundling debris out of the hole onto the spoil heap below.

Whenever I leaned over to look closer the face retreated into the burrow. At one time there were five standing in their burrow entrances.

I thought I had seen a green woodpecker last night, but then I thought as there aren't any trees up here it can't be. But this morning I got a good view of it, the low sun brought out the colour. I remembered that green woodpeckers are avid ant-eaters and so they do occur on heathland.

THREE LEAFLETS—CINQUEFOIL HAS FIVE

FOUR PETALS, CINQUEFOIL HAS FIVE

A large hive-bee was in two minds as to whether it should visit the top of my water container or the tormentil, both are the same colour.

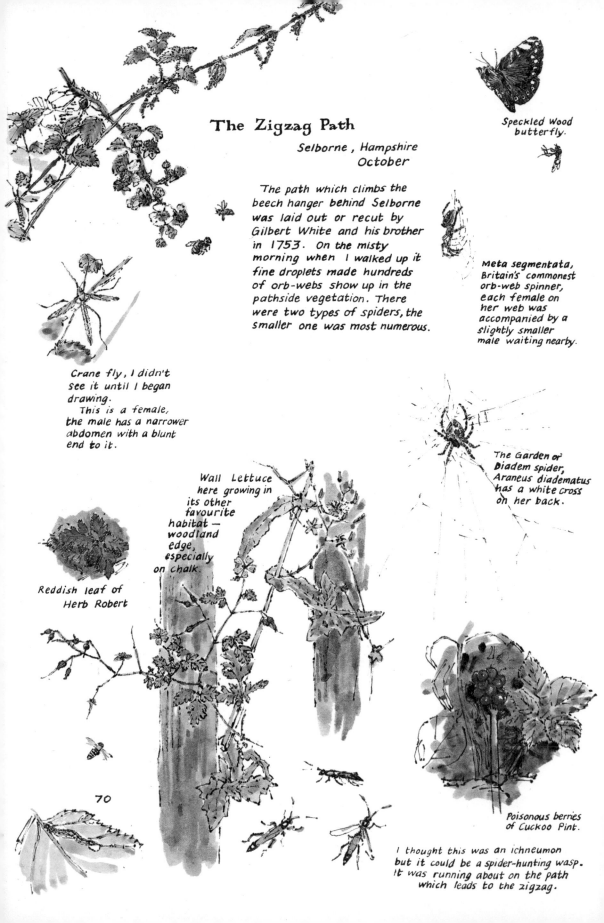

The Zigzag Path

Selborne, Hampshire
October

Speckled Wood butterfly.

The path which climbs the beech hanger behind Selborne was laid out or recut by Gilbert White and his brother in 1753. On the misty morning when I walked up it fine droplets made hundreds of orb-webs show up in the pathside vegetation. There were two types of spiders, the smaller one was most numerous.

Meta segmentata, Britain's commonest orb-web spinner, each female on her web was accompanied by a slightly smaller male waiting nearby.

Crane fly, I didn't see it until I began drawing.
This is a female, the male has a narrower abdomen with a blunt end to it.

The Garden or Diadem spider, Araneus diadematus has a white cross on her back.

Wall Lettuce here growing in its other favourite habitat — woodland edge, especially on chalk.

Reddish leaf of Herb Robert

70

Poisonous berries of Cuckoo Pint.

I thought this was an ichneumon but it could be a spider-hunting wasp. It was running about on the path which leads to the zigzag.

The white
c-shape
gives the
butterfly
its name.

The underwing is
coloured so as to
resemble a tattered
leaf.

I think being a country parson in Jane Austen's England would have suited me very well. It was interesting to see where White lived and made his natural history observations. His writing hasn't dated, it remains fresh, free of the affected mannerisms of some of Jane Austen's characters and his clear handwriting is much easier to read than the stylish copperplate of the period.

Roe deer making off along the woodland ride and into the trees.

Sipping the juice of ripe black-berries this is the first Comma I've seen; up in Yorkshire they are rare or absent.

A weasel appeared on the fallen beech – no it was a stoat, I didn't get a good look at it but it was about the size of the squirrels and it had the black tip to its tail. After remaining motionless for some moments it shot off along, behind, round and back as if trying to ambush a squirrel that might be hiding on the fallen tree.

The drawings on this page were made in a wood a mile or two south east of Selborne.

On the path on the sunny bank of a woodland ride there was the shiny translucent sloughed skin of a snake.

14-spot ladybird

Beech-Tuft fungus is entirely white, the caps glossy with slime.

Bracket fungus Ganoderma applanatum growing from beech roots.

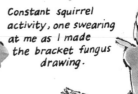

Constant squirrel activity, one swearing at me as I made the bracket fungus drawing.

Beech mast, gnawed open and ripe.

A roadside casualty.
Looking through a moth book is like looking at hundreds of Persian carpets. I thought this was a Noctuid, a member of a big group of 'moth-like' moths, but I'm 99% sure that it is the Frosted Orange, one of the Geometers. Most Geometers are butterfly-like but a few are stouter & moth-like.

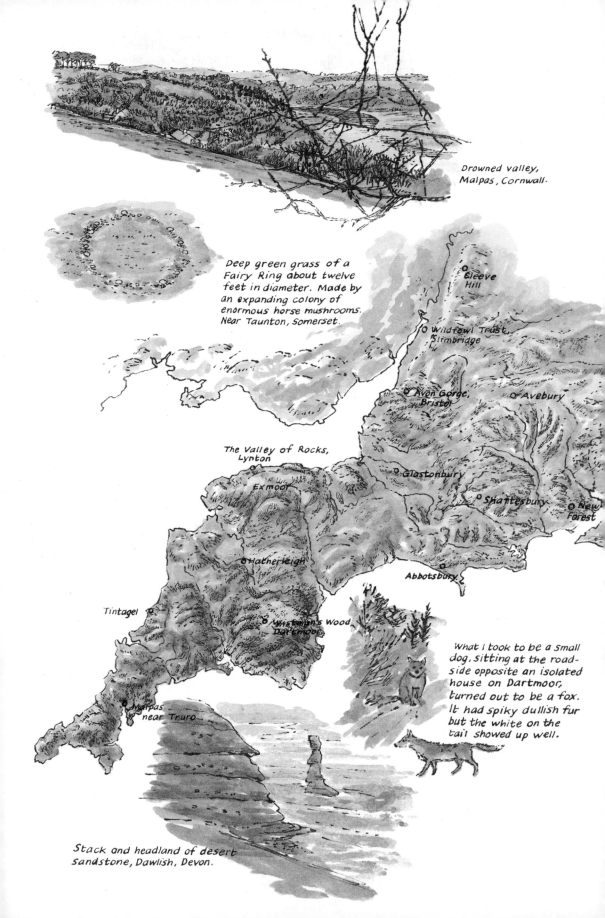

Drowned valley,
Malpas, Cornwall.

Deep green grass of a
Fairy Ring about twelve
feet in diameter. Made by
an expanding colony of
enormous horse mushrooms.
Near Taunton, Somerset.

Cleeve
Hill

Wildfowl Trust
Slimbridge

Avon Gorge,
Bristol

Avebury

The Valley of Rocks,
Lynton

Glastonbury

Exmoor

Shaftesbury

New
Forest

Hatherleigh

Abbotsbury

Tintagel

Wistman's Wood
Dartmoor

What I took to be a small
dog, sitting at the road-
side opposite an isolated
house on Dartmoor,
turned out to be a fox.
It had spiky dullish fur
but the white on the
tail showed up well.

Malpas
near Truro

Stack and headland of desert
sandstone, Dawlish, Devon.

THE WEST COUNTRY

October–February

I had already seen something of the West Country while painting the
New Forest after my trip to Selborne and the Isle of Wight, but my first
real visit to what I think of as Wessex wasn't until October. I went by
coach from Bath – a slow, roundabout journey that took me past many of
the places I most associate with the area. We climbed up and over the
Mendip Hills, wound down and across the Somerset levels, by Wells and
its cathedral, along narrowing lanes past Glastonbury Tor as the sun set,
and then into the chalk hills of Dorset. In the twilight I could just make
out the rude giant cut into the hillside turf above Cerne Abbas. The coach
finally stopped at Dorchester, the Casterbridge of Thomas Hardy's novels,
from where I went on to explore the coast at Abbotsbury and the
countryside around Shaftesbury.

I visited the West Country on several occasions between October and
February. As autumn turned to winter, each visit brought increasingly
dramatic weather. In late October I spent three days on Dartmoor, with
hardly a break in the rain. One of the first things I discovered, soon after
I got off the bus at Moretonhampstead, was that my anorak was not
waterproof – at least not against the shower-bath conditions I encountered
on the eight-mile walk up the moor to Postbridge. I tried thumbing a lift,
but no one seemed very keen to pick up a cold and soaking hitch-hiker.
I've learned my lesson, however. Now I always take a waterproof kagoule
on expeditions as well as an anorak.

Each morning on Dartmoor I set off early from my bed and breakfast for
Wistman's wood. By about halfway there a few raindrops would be
spotting down, gradually increasing to a shower and finally a relentless
downpour just as I reached the trees. I spent most of the time crouching
uncomfortably under a massive granite boulder, the only shelter available.
Drawing was almost impossible – every time I made a mark on the paper

a drop of water would trickle down the rock above me and plop onto the page. Squatting there, with the rain lashing about me and the ancient oaks, shaggy with fern and lichen, swaying crazily in the wind, I began to wonder if my ideal of always drawing from nature was really such a good one. But I decided that I would rather be out experiencing the country at first hand than stuck in a studio in London trying to recreate hedgerows and rabbits from photographs and drawings. Perhaps I could have taken a few small things – a branch covered with moss, a piece of granite – back with me to draw indoors, but I doubt they would have given much of an impression of this extraordinary place.

I was staying not far from Dartmoor prison. In the evenings, as I walked into Princetown near by for a meal, the cell blocks with their rows of lights and barred windows stood out gaunt and dark against the clouds sweeping by low overhead. The scene was like a Turner seascape of men-of-war at night, and in fact the prison was built to house French prisoners during the Napoleonic Wars. But with no prospect of the weather improving – the rain can set in on Dartmoor for a fortnight at a time – I decided to move on to the Wildfowl Trust at Slimbridge in Gloucestershire. There you can draw the geese and ducks in comfort from behind a plate-glass window.

But for me the most interesting aspect of the West Country is its coastal scenery. One of the best ways to see it is to go by train along the line that follows the red cliffs of Devon between Exmouth and Teignmouth, tunnelling through headlands from one bay to the next with one or two isolated stacks just offshore. The redness of the rocks here suggests that this area must once have been a desert, with the occasional flash flood or swollen river depositing the pebbly debris you can see packed into the strata.

Further south, in Cornwall, the coast indicates development of a different kind. There are massive blocks of granite as on Dartmoor, but the cliffs also contain layers of rock contorted, baked and compressed to form slates. Cornwall was probably part of Africa at one time, and the granite was formed when Africa collided with Britain and Europe some 300 million years ago. Rocks trapped between the two continents were intensely folded to form mountains in whose roots crystals – shiny flakes of mica, translucent quartz and white or pink oblongs of feldspar – appeared as the liquid rock cooled deep underground.

I took the train to Cornwall in December when I visited Tintagel. Gale-force winds and squalls of icy rain were buffeting the castle headland, which made drawing difficult, but it was by far the most spectacular weather in which to see this stretch of coast. In places water was pouring over the edge of the cliffs, to hang in the air as a cloud of silver droplets suspended by the wind gusting up from below. Sheltering behind a crag I put away my sketchbook and instead sat and watched the sea. Whipped up by a hard southwest wind huge waves funnelled into the bay, pounding the cliffs with a deep, drawn-out boom. Sheets of green water shot into the air and then disintegrated against the rockface, throwing off clouds of spray. The veins of white quartz which crisscrossed the rock looked yellowish compared to the snowy foam.

The scale of the place was awesome. The waves moved so slowly that I began to lose all sense of time and place. A tiny speck far down below in the bay looked like a fluttering sparrow, but turned out to be a pied pigeon. A fulmar showed up charcoal grey against the white froth of the sea; a flock of herring gulls perched on the cliffs resembled melting snow or frozen spray. Looking down from the gallery in the Albert Hall I've often felt there would be room for our house in the auditorium below. In the bay of Tintagel there would have been room for the entire Albert Hall.

After the storms and turbulence of Tintagel the next place I went to see, Truro, was calm and sheltered, even in February. Here and at Malpas near by I found I was able to work out of doors for almost the whole day. Like most of Devon and Cornwall, Truro is protected by the Gulf Stream from the colder weather of the north and east. This creates a warm, wet climate that influences plant life greatly, for instance lichens grow far more luxuriantly on western coasts. On the other hand, a Dartmoor farmer told me that because of the damp barley and oats grown on the moor were very susceptible to diseases such as rusts and smuts. The West Country climate seems to favour dairy farming, with sheep and ponies on the granite uplands.

Although the wind and rain often made it hard for me to use my sketch-book, late autumn and winter are the most exciting times of the year to see this part of the country. But there was one drawback. Gales and rough seas wash pollution ashore, and at Tintagel I saw an almost routine example of oil lying on the beach in sticky porridge-like lumps. This not only ruins the beaches that attract so many holidaymakers, it seriously affects marine life, particularly seabirds. Yet suppose that mess on the beach had been plutonium instead of oil.

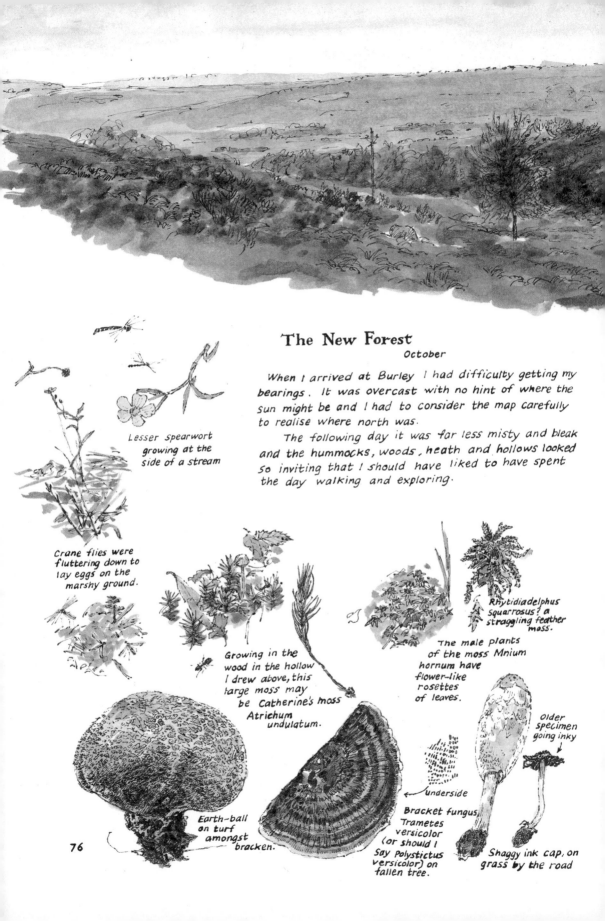

The New Forest

October

When I arrived at Burley I had difficulty getting my bearings. It was overcast with no hint of where the sun might be and I had to consider the map carefully to realise where north was.

The following day it was far less misty and bleak and the hummocks, woods, heath and hollows looked so inviting that I should have liked to have spent the day walking and exploring.

Lesser spearwort growing at the side of a stream

Crane flies were fluttering down to lay eggs on the marshy ground.

Growing in the wood in the hollow I drew above, this large moss may be Catherine's moss *Atrichum undulatum*.

Rhytidiadelphus Squarrosus? a straggling feather moss.

The male plants of the moss *Mnium hornum* have flower-like rosettes of leaves.

Older specimen going inky

← underside

Earth-ball on turf amongst bracken.

Bracket fungus *Trametes versicolor* (or should I say *Polystictus versicolor*) on fallen tree.

Shaggy ink cap, on grass by the road

Wheatear on heathy
ground, most have
migrated south by
now and the male
has taken on a
browner buffish
plumage similar to
that of the female.

This cross-section of the sandy
soil of the New Forest, exposed
at an old railway embankment,
shows why heathland soil is so
poor in minerals. Rain drains
rapidly through the sand
taking soluble minerals with
it. These are deposited in a
hard rusty layer lower down.
  Bracken does well on such
poor soils. The plant contains
silica, the glassy material of
flint and sand. The ash
contains over 40% silica
(according to an analysis in
A Potter's Book by Bernard
Leach) and it can be made
into a glaze for pottery.

Boletus scaber
grows in partnership
with birch and other
trees, the mycelium
forms a sheath round
the roots of the tree.

77

Cotswold stone wall

Cleeve Hill
October

Even in this small stretch of wall there are several distinct habitats. Flowering ivy grows from the wall top amongst branches of orchard trees. The face of the wall is sprinkled with lichens and over it grows the non-flowering climbing form of ivy (the same plant but a different leaf-shape). Mosses only grow lower down where there is more muck and hence more nutrients. Probably it is damper here too. On the trampled ground at the foot of the wall there is an assortment of wasteground plants.

And there's a further dimension; in the limestone are fragmentary fossils from a warm Jurassic sea.

Creeping thistle and nettles grow against the wall. Both are plants of disturbed ground and are reasonably resistant to grazing.

Froghopper

Harvestmen patrolled the foot of the wall...

16 legs in violent battle...

...yet they look so delicate. The one with the fly made off into a cranny in the wall. How had it caught it? I could just make it out in the gloom with the victim. All that was missing was the demonic echoing laugh.

Odd... the rest of the flock were up the hill & this one was on its own wearing a natty red collar. After munching a windfall it began sampling my thermos flask and haversack. When I'd finished work and was striding back down the track it came running after me.

78

Ivy coming into flower attracting flies, beetles, bees and late butterflies.

Shell fragments fossilised in the limestone.

Lair of a wall spider, Amaurobius Similis(?)

The white lichen was Lecanora calcarea, common on limestone. The yellow one probably Caloplaca heppiana, again a lichen of limestone, also found on cement. There were small sooty marks, another lime-loving lichen, Verrucaria nigrescens (I think).

Thistle seed?

Close-up of Cotswold limestone; the round pellets are known as ooids because of their resemblance to fish roe (oon is Greek for egg). They were formed of calcite in shallow waters and are rounded because of continual agitation by tidal currents.

There are some small fragments of shell amongst the ooids.

At the foot of the wall Bryum argenteum, a moss common on rocks and on pavement edges in towns, seems to favour nitrogen rich conditions.

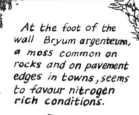

Pineapple weed

Annual meadow grass

Greater Plantain

Chickweed

Tangle of plants at the trackside at the foot of the wall. All are prolific producers of seed and quickly colonise disturbed ground and they can all tolerate a considerable amount of trampling.

79

Abbotsbury

Dorset, October

Sun ray motif on the cap of this fungus growing on the pasture by St Catherine's Chapel. Could it be Coprinus plicatilis which 'Observer's Fungi' neatly describes as 'resembling a miniature Japanese umbrella'?

My brother told me of the 100 or so pairs of swans had seen in July nesting at the swannery. I decided do a page of close-up studies but by this time of t year the swans have moved on and can be seen feedin half-way along the lagoon called the Fleet which backs Chesil beach. I spent the morning walking there. A hunt surrounded a patch of bushy hill-side, perhaps digging a fox out.

Bolbitius vitellinus grows on dung. It seems that the spores can pass through the digestive system of a cow or horse.

The stone beneath which I found the snail had marks on it which resembled splatters in mud.

Rusty limestone full of debris which includes shell fragments & sections of sea-lily stems

The shell of this small snail was semi-transparent and covered with glistening bristles.

It looks like Ponentina subvirescens, the green hairy snail, which lives on grassy and rocky slopes near the sea. If so it is on the edge of its range here because in Britain it is only to be found on the south-west coasts of England.

Track of snail across the page

80

Kestrel chased by crows.

A view from Abbotsbury looking down the sixteen mile length of Chesil beach to Portland Bill. The Portland stone which makes up this headland is a continuation of the ridge of Jurassic limestone that forms Lincoln Edge and the Cotswolds. I have taken this outcrop, which crosses England diagonally, as dividing the midlands and the west country from the English lowlands.

The first buzzard I have seen on this expedition, putting up rooks and pigeons over a wood. I feel I'm entering western Britain.

At midday I arrived at a stubble field from which I could see more than eighty swans feeding on the Fleet. But I only had time to draw the green hairy snail before a squall of rain came in over the sea. For shelter I crouched by a solitary bale of straw and drank my flask of coffee. On top of the bale were grey droppings, probably a fox marking its territory.

Last days of summer for the flies — and I've scarcely looked at them. The spot-winged one with long legs has a tendency to do press-ups. What a design — more functions than a snooze-alarm wrist-watch.

The Chinese Chusan Palm in Abbotsbury's sub-tropical gardens. I thought I would allow myself a touch of the exotic since I have been drawing so much British wildlife recently.

81

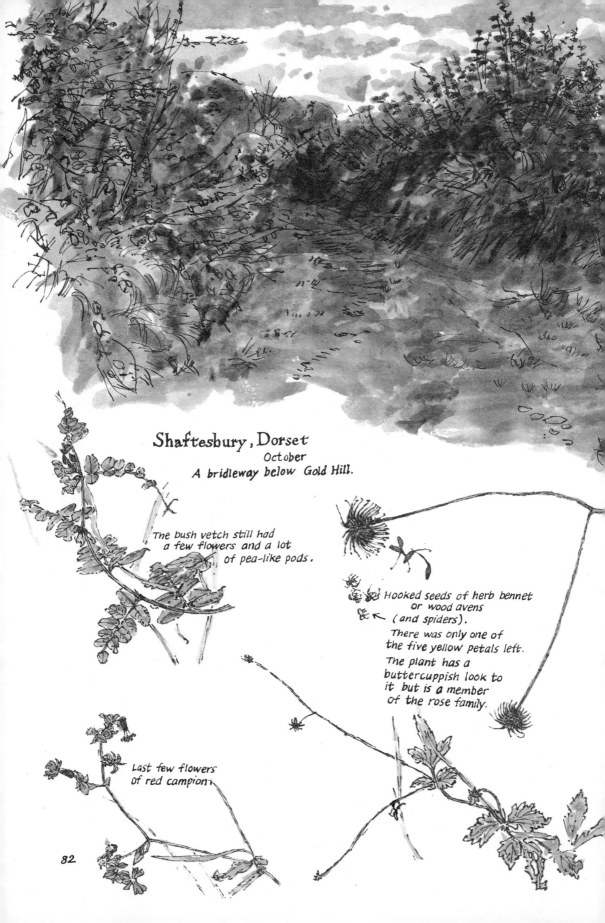

Shaftesbury, Dorset
October
A bridleway below Gold Hill.

The bush vetch still had
a few flowers and a lot
of pea-like pods.

Hooked seeds of herb bennet
or wood avens
(and spiders).

There was only one of
the five yellow petals left.

The plant has a
buttercuppish look to
it but is a member
of the rose family.

Last few flowers
of red campion

82

Despite what I say there the hedge does have an under-lying structure—

A BACKBONE OF HAWTHORN, ELDER & HAZEL
CLIMBERS SUCH AS BRAMBLES & VETCH
HERB LAYER OF CAMPION, HERB BENNET ETC
& ON THE DISTURBED GROUND ALONGSIDE OPPORTUNISTS LIKE NETTLES, DOCKS, DANDELION & GREAT PLANTAIN

Cézanne had an idea that nature consists of spheres, cones and cylinders. Well, I expect nature is based on geometry in close-up, in the structure of a leaf or a snail shell and in the distance trees and outcrops of rock have geometric forms. It's in the middle-distance that there are complications. There is so much randomness that the pattern is lost. That's why I find tangles of vegetation so difficult to draw; how can I be selective and simplify randomness? Why should I want to? In nature the 'background noise' is as important as the 'message'. The universe may be comparatively simple and homogeneous at the scale of expanding galaxies and at the atomic scale but much of the interest lies in knots of complexity in between.

83

As I sat amongst the thistles and nettles
and began drawing a kestrel appeared
hovering over the flat top of Silbury Hill.

84

Fool's
watercress

Seven-
spot ladybird
on nettle

Water
speedwell

AVEBURY
October

In medieval times there was quite an industry in breaking up and burying the stones of the circle and avenues at Avebury.

Ant's wing from Silbury Hill compared with modern example.

But the stone I've drawn in the foreground above fell prematurely into the pit that had been dug for it. When the stone was excavated in the 1930's the skeleton of a man was found trapped beneath it. The scissors and probe in what had been his purse suggest he was a barber-surgeon and coins of Edward I show that he died in the 1300's.

At the core of Silbury Hill is a turf-covered mound. The turf has been preserved and amongst the grass (which has been grazed, probably by cattle) are the remains of beetles and other insects. The radio-carbon date of 2260 BC is only correct to within about 400 years but there is a clue to the month that construction started. Ants found in the turf have wings so it must have been during August when the mating flights take place.

Winged dragon carved on the medieval font in Avebury church. In an entertaining book called 'The Mysteries of Chartres Cathedral' Louis Charpentier points out that winged serpents were used as a symbol of currents which snake through the ground. Megalithic monuments, he says, are associated with these currents.

85

Avon Gorge
October

Obviously I'm happier drawing umbels than
bridges. But I felt I couldn't come here and
not draw the bridge; to do it justice I should
have let it span these two pages but then
there'd be no room to show the plants that
grow at the top of the limestone cliff nearby.

As I write this there are eight
jackdaws on the bridge pier nearest me.
This morning a pair came so close that
I could see the yellow of their eyes.

Small scabious,
a plant of
chalk &
limestone banks.
The leaves are more finely
divided than those of common
scabious.

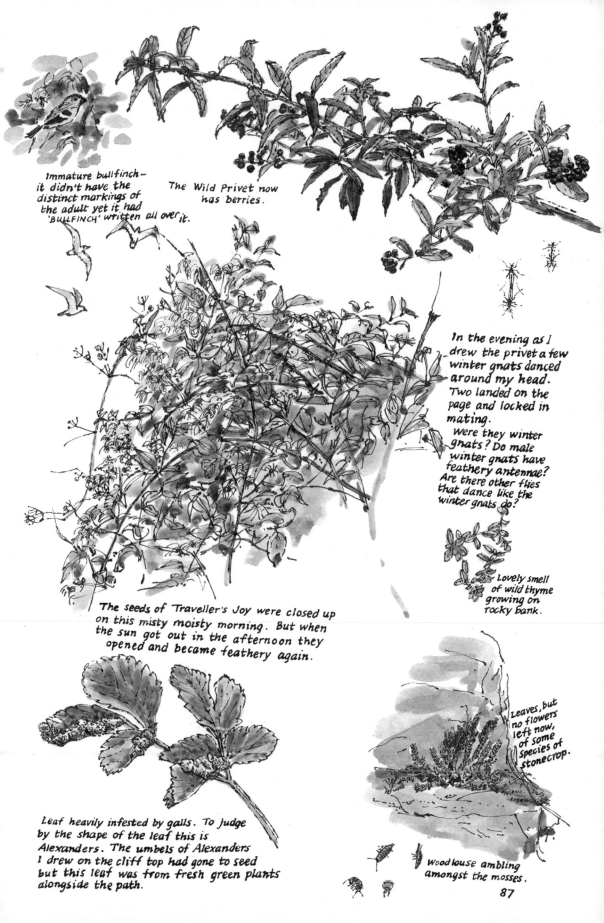

Immature bullfinch—
it didn't have the
distinct markings of
the adult yet it had
'BULLFINCH' written all over it.

The Wild Privet now
has berries.

In the evening as I
drew the privet a few
winter gnats danced
around my head.
Two landed on the
page and locked in
mating.
Were they winter
gnats? Do male
winter gnats have
feathery antennae?
Are there other flies
that dance like the
winter gnats do?

Lovely smell
of wild thyme
growing on
rocky bank.

The seeds of Traveller's Joy were closed up
on this misty moisty morning. But when
the sun got out in the afternoon they
opened and became feathery again.

Leaves, but
no flowers
left now,
of some
species of
stonecrop.

Leaf heavily infested by galls. To judge
by the shape of the leaf this is
Alexanders. The umbels of Alexanders
I drew on the cliff top had gone to seed
but this leaf was from fresh green plants
alongside the path.

Woodlouse ambling
amongst the mosses.

87

Buzzard circling more rapidly than usual in a strong breeze.

BROWN, SO IT WAS A JUVENILE.

A cormorant flying along the line of the Blackbrook river wasn't what I'd expect to see in the middle of Dartmoor. Had the rainstorm blown it off course? No, there it was the next day about the same time (2.30 pm) flying west again.

Rain-soaked drawing of Littaford Tors above Wistman's wood.

Granite wasn't laid down in strata like a sedimentary rock, but it does have a system of cracks and joints. These formed parallel to the surface of the mass of molten granite as it cooled deep underground.

During the ice age the high tors of Dartmoor stood above the ice sheets and they were subjected to severe erosion. Water expanding as it froze in vertical crevices had the power to push huge blocks of the rock sideways. Boulders slid down the slope during thaws when the ground turned to slushy mud. Jumbles of granite boulders are locally known as 'clitter.' Wistman's wood grows on clitter in the West Dart valley in the centre of the moor.

Dung beetle, Geotrupes, making thoughtful progress over my anorak, pausing to rub its head with its combed forearm.

Stoat skipping from rock to rock. A squirrel-like movement.

Rugged walls of Dartmoor granite support not only mosses and lichens but also ferns, grasses and gorse and, on this garden wall, foxglove and feverfew (bachelor's buttons)!

Wistman's Wood

Dartmoor September

The oaks are gnarled and stunted, festooned with lichen, mosses, ferns and even bilberry. The wood has the atmosphere of being one of the loneliest places on Earth... but not this morning. You must need nerves of steel to bring a school party out here!

Big guns were thumping, the red flag was up on Beardown Tor.

If the robins had a summer recess in order to moult it is over now, they are calling and disputing vigorously.

Female

A male seizes the trapped fly.

His rival leaves the female's web and shelters from the rain.

Male embraces the female.

Tiac Taac
Tac
Tac
Tac

A movement caught my eye; a dull-coloured dung-fly had fallen into a loose spiral orb-web and a spider rushed out to take it. This was a female, there were two smaller males waiting at the edge of the web, they had disproportionately long front legs. To my surprise one of them came out as if to seize the fly. Not a wise move as the female is so much bigger, however she backed off. But he soon had her in an embrace and then those extra-long legs came in useful as he tapped her on the back and began the rather dangerous manoeuvre of mating.

89

At first many of the geese were
on the water. After half an hour
they were back on the grass and
they preened for an hour. Now
most of them are grazing.
They move as a flock.

Drinking

I find it remarkable that a creature with
such high energy demands as a bird should
feed almost exclusively on grass — which
can't have a very high octane rating.

Slimbridge

Gloucestershire,
November.
Barnacle geese at
the Wildfowl Trust.

Eventually the whole lot of them
trailed over to the other pond.

Whooper swan – as large
as the mute but with
yellow on the bill, which
hasn't a knob on it.
← Doesn't hold in neck
in the familiar S-shape
of the mute.

91

Bryn and Cefn Cyff, lower outliers of the Beacons.

Brecon Beacons   *November*

After so long exploring the lowlands it's good to reach the mountains of highland Britain. The dramatic north facing scarp of Brecon Beacons was invisible in the mist and lashing rain and I spent my first day getting soaked and drawing from the shelter of bridges on the by-pass which is under construction.

But the next day was perfect and the Mountain Centre provided the most comfortable conditions I've ever had for drawing a landscape.

The highest points on the Beacons scarp Pen Y Fan 2,706 feet 6 inches (886 metres) and Corn Dû. The low sun emphasised the texture of the slopes — crags, screes, bracken and woodland.

The Beacons are topped by tough gritty sandstones known as the Plateau Beds.

A loud splash and a fish the size of an otter leapt up. Trout?

The Afon Tarrel.
Opposite me a drain let
out reddish water. The soils
here are derived from the
Old Red Sandstone. 93

The Valley of Rocks

A mass of ice filled the Bristol Channel during the most severe of the glaciations of the last two million years. Torrents that would have flowed directly into the Bristol Channel from the Exmoor plateau now had to flow along the edge of the ice until they found an escape route to the south. This seems to be the origin of the Valley of Rocks which runs parallel to the steep coastline west of Lynton.

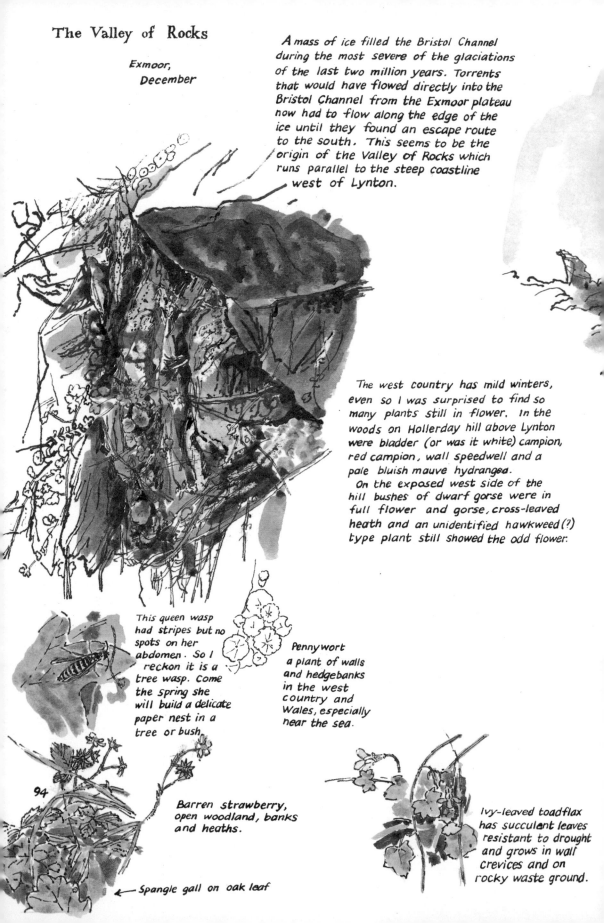

The west country has mild winters, even so I was surprised to find so many plants still in flower. In the woods on Hollerday hill above Lynton were bladder (or was it white) campion, red campion, wall speedwell and a pale bluish mauve hydrangea.
On the exposed west side of the hill bushes of dwarf gorse were in full flower and gorse, cross-leaved heath and an unidentified hawkweed (?) type plant still showed the odd flower.

This queen wasp had stripes but no spots on her abdomen. So I reckon it is a tree wasp. Come the spring she will build a delicate paper nest in a tree or bush.

Pennywort a plant of walls and hedgebanks in the west country and Wales, especially near the sea.

94

Barren strawberry, open woodland, banks and heaths.

Ivy-leaved toadflax has succulent leaves resistant to drought and grows in wall crevices and on rocky waste ground.

← Spangle gall on oak leaf

95

The Valley of Rocks from the shelter of a small pavilion,
though the wind was blowing so strongly that the rain came
in at 70 degrees.

Glastonbury

Somerset
December

It's not impossible that the 5th or 6th century British chieftain King Arthur was buried in the cemetery of the original monastery. Edward I and Eleanor (she's the one commemorated by the cross at Charing Cross) had the remains reinterred in the quire of the Abbey with great ceremony.

The pub which at first glance seemed a Victorian revival turned out to be genuine – it was standing when Henry VII visited the Abbey. It must be unique among pubs in still having a notice 'Hippies not admitted.'

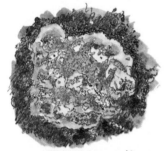

This lichen on the limestone Abbey wall looks like *Caloplaca aurantia*. The older darker patches are cracked into granular crazy-paving.

In some stones in the walls there were fossil belemnites, the inner shells of creatures that were forerunners of cuttlefish and squids.

Different types of stone were used in the building of the Abbey, a fine-grained limestone from Caen in Normandy was used for detailed carving. Tufa, a very light stone that forms in a similar way to the scaling of kettles in hard water areas, was used in the vaulted ceilings.

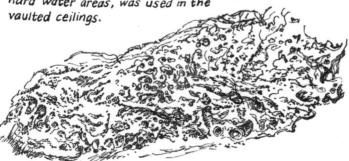

96

Coral (?) in limestone wall.

On the Glastonbury Thorn in the abbey grounds there were scattered blossoms, blossoms in bud, dying leaves, unfurling leaves as well as, as you might expect in December, ripe haws.

Enthusiastic bubbling and cackling from the starlings and a robin sang from one of the top branches — a clear reedy voice.

Blue tit investigating twigs for insect life.

The sands and clays that make up the Tor at Glastonbury were laid down in warm seas during the Jurassic period about 170 million years ago. The Tor is an outlier of the Jurassic scarp which crosses England diagonally. These same sands and clays, capped by limestone, form Lincoln edge.

The Tor overlooks the Somerset levels, the original sediments of the levels were probably deposited in a lake which formed when ice blocked the Bristol Channel.

Tintagel

December

This watery sketch of the church on the cliff top is all I had time to do before the rain set in. Gales continued throughout the following day. The wind speed gauge at the local RAF station went off the dial — and the dial goes up to 120 mph. Few houses in Tintagel escaped damage, even the church had gaping holes in its roof. A goat was found still safe in its field but the shed it lived in had vanished without trace.

Further down the coast a Greek freighter, the Skopelos Sky , broke up in heavy seas.

Next day there were fifty barrels of lubricating oil washed up on the rocks below the castle with another eighty floating amongst the breakers. In Merlin's Cave I found eight barrels still intact. But many had broken open — the water was opaque, a milky slurry laced with black oil instead of the snowy foam of previous days. Rocks were covered with black frothy scum. Instead of a taste of salt in the air there was a disgusting taste of oil. A greyish porridge scattered over the pebbles stuck to my boots and was very difficult to scrape off.

Sea spleenwort growing by a rock near the castle.

The bay below Tintagel castle from the partial shelter of Merlin's cave. I was surprised there was such a draught blowing out of it but in fact the cave extends right under the island.

On the day of the gales (when drawing was impossible) the waves exploded in slow motion engulfing the 200 foot high cliffs in white water.

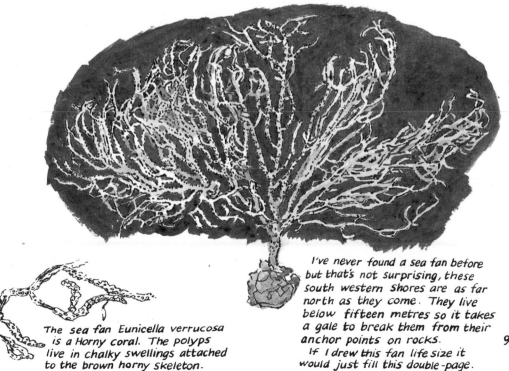

The sea fan Eunicella verrucosa is a Horny coral. The polyps live in chalky swellings attached to the brown horny skeleton.

I've never found a sea fan before but that's not surprising, these south western shores are as far north as they come. They live below fifteen metres so it takes a gale to break them from their anchor points on rocks.

If I drew this fan life size it would just fill this double-page.

99

On this stretch of estuary,
between the two large pines in
front of me, I can count:

45 shelduck

79 black-headed gulls — some
now with chocolate heads.

4 redshank — perhaps more,
they don't show up well
against the mud.

4 curlew — very conspicuous
by their calls.

2 herring gulls — one of them
immature

2 teal

The mud must be teeming with
life to support such a collection
of birds, all with their different
methods of feeding.

Ten sanderlings were feeding along
the water's edge amongst gulls.
A very similar looking bird was
indulging in tail-bobbing — sandpiper?
Suddenly there were 125-30
sanderlings. They flew in, light-
winged.

Redshank probing the mud
then joining the gulls and
preening vigorously.

Dead woodlouse on
the granite water-
side steps. The long
tail gave it the look
of a shrimp.
A sea slater.

100

On the edge of the granite steps,
swaying with the ebbing tide. Then
a scum of oil floated over it so I
was unable to continue the drawing.

Knotted
wrack

Rough stippled
surface.

Malpas

near Truro, Cornwall
February

The channels in the mud remind me of a sinuous Chinese dragon.

Truro River occupies a drowned valley. During the Ice Age so much water became locked-up in extensive ice-sheets that sea level dropped to at least 135 metres below its present height. Rivers cut their way down to the new shore line. When the ice melted and the seas rose these valleys were flooded.

Here at Malpas Truro River looks broad at high tide but it shrinks to become a narrow channel at low tide.

A balletic clockwork movement. Yes, it is a Common sandpiper.

This massive drystone wall is built of chunks of 'killas', the local name for rock which was baked and altered by a molten mass of granite as it rose towards the surface. The veins of white quartz were sweated out of the rock by this event.

When this took place, about 280 million years ago, Britain was becoming locked at the arid heart of the super-continent Pangea. The intense pressures of a continental collision may have caused the granite-melt.

The dandelions growing on this wall have exceptionally deeply indented, finely divided leaves.

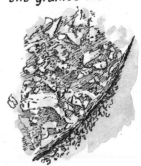

On the path through woods to the water's edge, the first celandine I've seen in flower — in Yorkshire only the leaves are showing at present.

The granite pavements of Truro shone dazzlingly after a heavy shower. The granite contained lots of massive white feldspar crystals up to 2 or 3 centimetres long. The slower a molten rock cools the bigger the crystals, this granite must have cooled slowly in the roots of a mountain chain. But the feldspar crystals continued growing as mineral-rich water made its way outwards from the cooling granite mass.

101

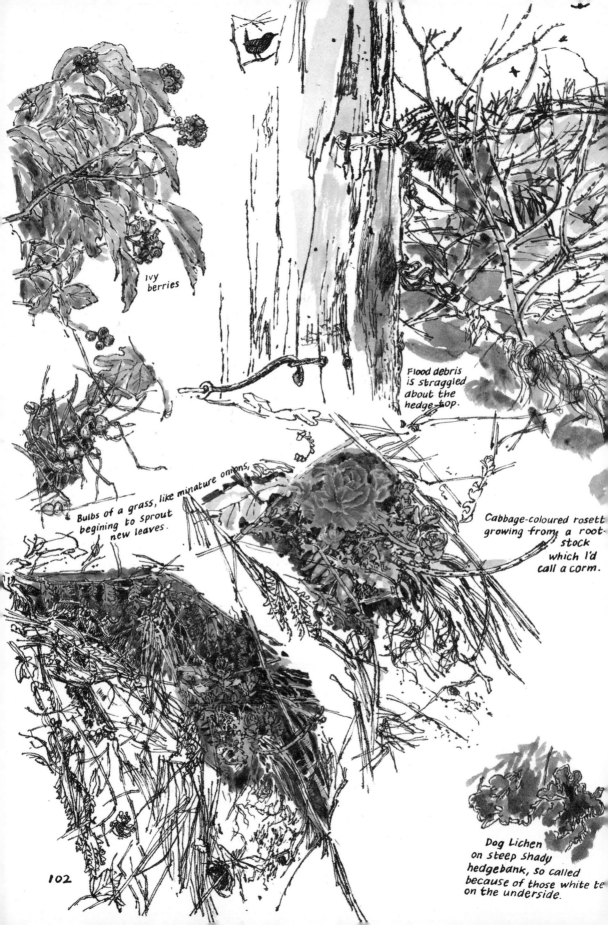

Ivy berries

Flood debris is straggled about the hedge top.

Bulbs of a grass, like miniature onions, begining to sprout new leaves.

Cabbage-coloured rosette growing from a root-stock which I'd call a corm.

Dog Lichen on steep shady hedgebank, so called because of those white te on the underside.

102

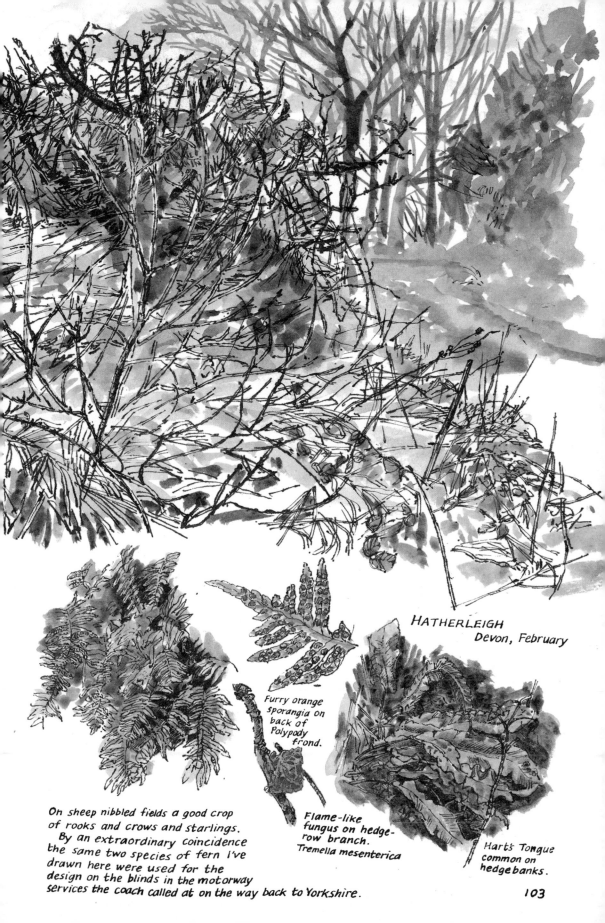

HATHERLEIGH
Devon, February

Furry orange
sporangia on
back of
Polypody
frond.

On sheep nibbled fields a good crop
of rooks and crows and starlings.
  By an extraordinary coincidence
the same two species of fern I've
drawn here were used for the
design on the blinds in the motorway
services the coach called at on the way back to Yorkshire.

Flame-like
fungus on hedge-
row branch.
Tremella mesenterica

Hart's Tongue
common on
hedge banks.

103

Chester Zoo

Macclesfield

Millstone Grit wall,
Hathersage churchyard.

Charnwood
Forest

The Long Mynd

Olton

Ludlow

Pendas Fen
(Pinvin)

Warrington

Country south of Birmingham
sketched from the coach.

THE MIDLANDS

March

As a contrast to the wild open spaces of the West Country, I decided
I would see what wildlife survived in the shadow of the concrete overpasses
of Spaghetti Junction. I'd read an unusual Nature Conservancy report
called *The Endless Village* which surveys the surprising variety of plants
and animals surviving and even thriving within the West Midlands
conurbation, even in the patches of wasteland between motorway and
factory. But Spaghetti Junction turned out to be a remote and difficult
place to reach on foot, so my exploration of Birmingham took the form
of a morning's walk along the towpath of a canal from Olton to the edge
of the built-up area outside Solihull.

Birmingham has a greater mileage of canals than Venice and is an ideal
place to see how wildlife has adapted to an urban habitat. Canals act as
long, thin nature reserves, bringing green walkways into the centre of
cities. As I walked along the towpath a pair of mallard got up, quacking,
in a silver spray of water. Two bullfinches made their way through the
tangled brambles and bushes by the path. It could almost have been a rural
scene, and yet lorries were roaring along the overpass near by and the
canal went under several roads busy with rush-hour traffic. Farther on,
some of the tall straight sycamores on the steep embankment had collapsed
into the water. It was green with algae.

When I reached the main street in Solihull I realised that I'd come to a
small town or village fossilised within the urban sprawl. There was an old
church and opposite it a half-timbered coaching inn. This is the area
described by Edith Holden in her *Nature Notes* of 1906, and to judge by
her description it has become impoverished as fields have been built over
and copses and hedges lost. But, as the Nature Conservancy report shows,
some plants and animals have now won a place for themselves in suburbia,
amongst factories and rubbish tips. Foxes and kestrels are regularly seen

even in city centres. In the suburban gardens of Olton I might have found plenty of birds and wild plants (weeds, the gardener would call them), but I would have felt rather conspicuous sitting on a wall drawing shepherd's purse and groundsel growing on somebody's rosebed.

Many other parts of the Midlands are no less industrial and suburban. When I set off by train from Leicester to Macclesfield on a heavily overcast afternoon the cooling towers of the power station near Loughborough had their heads in the clouds. This is the kind of day when the industrial Midlands remind me of the illustrations in the history books I read at school. One brick-built town connected with the next, there were old coal and industrial tips, flash ponds shone in dark, derelict wasteland and traditional bell-shaped kilns stood among blackened factories as the train reached the Potteries. On such a day this part of the West Midlands lives up to its name of the Black Country, although by a railway siding at Stoke-on-Trent I was surprised to see that the ground was white, as if there had been a sudden fall of snow, or a frost. China clay had probably been unloaded here – china clay, or kaolin, is weathered granite used in making porcelain and paper. It is mined in Dartmoor and parts of Cornwall, where white moonscapes mark the places from which it has been extracted. When I was there in the winter I saw one village north of St Austell where everything – walls, roofs, even bushes – was powdered with fine white dust. The sombre grey granite of the village houses did nothing to enliven the strangely forbidding scene.

Of course, not all of central England is built-up and industrialised. On my visit to Pinvin I walked by rows of pollarded willows and passed a weatherboarded watermill in some meadows by the Avon. I drew the nearby Bredon Hill when I was there and, in the other direction, the long ridge of the Malvern Hills. The vale is ten miles across at this point. A valley on this scale is unlikely to have been carved out by a river and a cross-section between Bredon and the Malverns in fact reveals a deep downfold in the Earth's surface. As this basin subsided it was gradually filled with different sorts of rock.

From Pinvin I went by train to Church Stretton in the heart of the Long Mynd, a journey which took me through the cathedral town of Worcester and towards the Malverns. At Malvern Link houses climbed halfway up the steep hillside. There was the merest touch of cloud on the summit. Having seen the bulk of these hills at close range, I appreciated the magnitude of the eruption that was to blow apart Mount St Helens in the summer. Describing this event one geologist likened it to blowing the Malverns off the map in one stroke. These hills overlooking the vale of Worcester are much older than the vale itself and are composed of limestone. After a tunnel the railway finally emerges at the Malvern Water factory where spring water that has percolated through the rock is bottled. In places the limestone strata are tipped on edge so as to resemble the flying buttresses of a medieval cathedral.

Church Stretton itself is a town at the foot of a small, deep valley which cuts into the Long Mynd. I had looked forward for some time to visiting the Long Mynd – both the name and the unusual rounded shape of the hills intrigued me. The rocks here are among the most ancient to be found in England and Wales. To me, this area has strong connections with Britain's pagan past, as does Pinvin. Caractacus made his last, unsuccessful stand against the Romans at a hill fort near here on Caer Caradoc and in Church Stretton I found a worn carving of a Saxon goddess set into the outside wall of the church, above a Norman archway. It may seem odd that a pagan earth mother should be incorporated into a Christian shrine, perhaps it was done on the basis of 'if you can't beat 'em'. But in fact the statue was above the north door on the shady, unlucky side of the building, the door through which coffins were carried.

When I visit somewhere new I like to study an Ordnance Survey map beforehand and then on arrival call in at a Post Office or shop to see what there is in the way of local guides. Church Stretton library had leaflets and information sheets and at Ludlow the bookshops were well stocked with imaginatively produced booklets on local history and geology. At Charnwood Forest I found some excellent publications giving background information on Bradgate Park and I was able to get further insights on the evolution of the area by visiting Leicester Museum.

Some of the most rewarding places I've visited do not, however, get a mention in guide books. Macclesfield, for instance, is near to the popular viewpoint of Alderney Edge and the Peak District National Park. Many people are not so lucky as to be within easy reach of such celebrated pieces of countryside, but wherever you are there is always plenty to see. At Macclesfield I found more than enough to draw along the short stretch of derelict railway I came across.

Black poplar

Olton West Midlands
(it used to be in Warwickshire)
March

From Olton I walked along the canal towpath past the Land Rover factory, between earthy embankments crammed with tall straight sycamores until I came out at fields with cattle and a motorway on the edge of the West Midlands conurbation.

It rained most of the day, the mud was deep and slushy, then clayey and sticky. So muddy that it looked like 'February fill-dyke' a Victorian painting, one of the muddiest ever painted, which hangs in Birmingham City Art Gallery.

In the museum there is a large relief model of the midlands, it shows a vast expanse of green lowlands crossed diagonally by scarps. Not a patch of sea in sight.

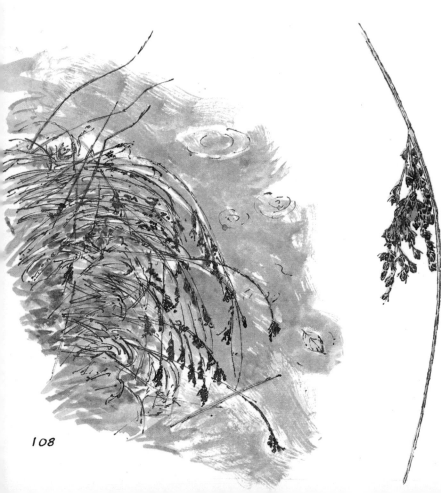

On the canal-side just beyond the Land Rovers, soft rush a plant of wet ground.

The view from my bed and breakfast, in a
large Victorian building only a hefty stone's-
throw from Gowan Bank, the house in
which Edith Holden was living when she
wrote and illustrated her Nature Notes
for 1906, published as the Country Diary of
an Edwardian Lady in 1977.
   There's a charm about the book that can't
now be recaptured, after the first world
war and all that followed. Besides you'd
have to cycle a lot further today to find
'quantities of Primroses and Sweet Violet
(both blue and white) on the banks of the
fields and on the roadside.'

109

It seems odd to be drawing a ready-mixed concrete depot when I'm in such a rural part of Britain, I'd intended to draw one of the pollarded willows by the river Avon. But it is cold, wet and rainy and the station shelter is the best place for me to draw from. Besides, this half-land has a wildness of its own.

Below, Bredon Hill in fading light. There is a plan to put a 'golf-ball' on the top; an early-warning radar like the ones on Fylingdales Moor in Yorkshire.

Penda's Fen Worcestershire March

The distant hills are the Malverns, seen here from the village of Pinvin. The name Pinvin means 'Penda's Fen', Penda of Mercia was the last pagan king in England. This dark ages connection was one of the themes of a filmed television play 'Penda's Fen' written by David Rudkin, shown years ago. It involved a journey across this landscape towards the far hills and made use of Elgar's music, particularly 'The Dream of Gerontius', music which has a special relationship with this part of the country.

A good use of media; you couldn't combine music, landscape and history more effectively. The weakness of the media is that, unlike music, painting and books you can't come back to it when you wish to.

I stood by the place where Elgar lived as a boy as I waited in Worcester, near the Cathedral, for the bus that would bring me here. The music shop is no longer there, but there is a plaque to show where it was.

As I drew I noticed that every plant is different to every other, some are bedraggled, some crowded with billiard-ball sprouts and some remind me of prehistoric trees, their stems patterned with scaly leaf-scars. There is so much variation in these plants which are bred to be identical and grown under uniform conditions; think of the variation in wild plants responding to diverse conditions.

My interest in drawing is in the individual plant and its struggle to survive, rather than the idealised type-specimen of botanical illustration.

111

The Long Mynd
Shropshire March

Amongst the wiry leaves of sheep's fescue grass and small rosettes of sheep's sorrel, this small fungus had been nibbled. Hygrophorus obrusseus?

Harebell (drawn in September).

When tongues of ice from the Irish Sea and Wales surrounded the Long Mynd some 20,000 years ago the plateau was subjected to tundra conditions and the hard ancient rocks were shattered by violent frost action. Gravelly deposits now blanket the hill tops and give rise to a steady supply of unusually pure water.

It is refreshing to see such a clear sparkling stream. Also it is delicious to listen to; gurgling, motorboating and in one place there was a repeated sequence of low notes, as if from a didgeridoo. When I put my hand into the stream where the noise was coming from I found a cone-shaped hollow. Air was trapped under the rushing water.

willow moss Fontinalis antipyretica var. gracilis.

Moss growing in a very well oxygenated position on the rock below the little waterfall I've drawn.

112

Carding Mill Valley, Church Stretton; drawn
on a return visit in September, as it had been
raining when I was here in March.
The rocks of the Long Mynd are some of
the oldest in England and Wales, laid down
over 700 million years ago. No fossils of the
primitive life-forms that existed at this
time have been found in these rocks. Earth
movements have folded the layers
dramatically and here they are almost
vertical, an outcrop looks like
a stone curtain.

I've never seen so many snowdrops
as here in the Old Rectory Wood.
They grow here thanks to the
enthusiasm of a rector who also
planted bamboo, rhododendrons and
azaleas.
It was drizzling so I drew this
lying on the slope with my kagoule
over my head as a makeshift tent.
But it rained faster, the leaves
became silvery with droplets and large
drops started trickling onto the page.
As I walked back to Church Stretton
a stormcock (mistle thrush) was
singing from a fir. The clear repeated
song is so evocative of spring rain.

Retracting
its head.

A leatherjacket on a
grass clump by the
stream. Although it
looks so much like
a caterpillar it had
no legs. At the end
of spring it will
pupate and emerge
two weeks later as
a Daddy-long-legs.
Leatherjackets feed
on roots and stems.
113

Ludlow — Shropshire — March

It was siling it down. So I went to the museum which is in the 18th century ButterCross which stands on the site of a medieval market cross. I sat at a mahogany table, of the time of George III (c.1780), to draw the trilobite.

Daimanites candatus
SILURIAN-Wenlock
Limestone, stream exposure
(449 728) near drive-way
leading to New House Farm
Bartington nr Ludlow
Donor: Mr Thomas 14th Sept 1963

Turret-like multi-lensed eyes. I can imagine it half-buried in the mud like a flounder, only the eyes showing.

The development of the eye is reckoned to be one of the most complex problems to explain in terms of evolution. Darwin admitted 'the eye to this day gives me a cold shudder.'

On television this week in the 'Life on Earth' film series there was a sequence about trilobites, the first creatures on earth to develop high-definition eyes. They even came up with an elegant solution to a problem of distortion by using a second lens.

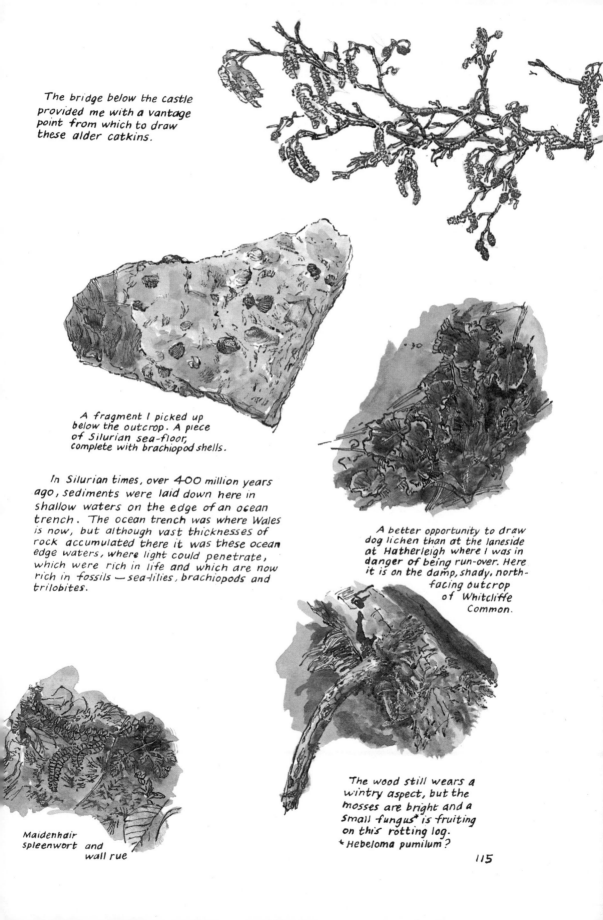

The bridge below the castle provided me with a vantage point from which to draw these alder catkins.

A fragment I picked up below the outcrop. A piece of Silurian sea-floor, complete with brachiopod shells.

In Silurian times, over 400 million years ago, sediments were laid down here in shallow waters on the edge of an ocean trench. The ocean trench was where Wales is now, but although vast thicknesses of rock accumulated there it was these ocean edge waters, where light could penetrate, which were rich in life and which are now rich in fossils — sea-lilies, brachiopods and trilobites.

A better opportunity to draw dog lichen than at the laneside at Hatherleigh where I was in danger of being run-over. Here it is on the damp, shady, north-facing outcrop of Whitcliffe Common.

The wood still wears a wintry aspect, but the mosses are bright and a small fungus* is fruiting on this rotting log.
* Hebeloma pumilum?

Maidenhair spleenwort and wall rue

Rhinoceros Iguana
Cyclura cornuta
Haiti and Puerto Rico

CHESTER ZOO March

When drawing living animals you are forced to be quick and decisive. This helps prevent work from becoming stodgy. Zoos are certainly good places to draw but I wonder about their conservation value. Chester has had many breeding successes but captive breeding is of limited value if habitats are disappearing for ever.

Male with cheek pouches.

Orang utan
Borneo and Sumatra

I feel I should be analysing structure when I'm drawing animals — sometimes that's not so easy.

116

Lowland
Gorilla
Africa

A repetitive
sequence of
movements round
the cage.

Mountain Gorilla
Africa

Iron & concrete,
a pity they can't
have more sympathetic
materials — though they
do have wood and grass
outside.

117

118

Fallow deer. One million people visit the park in a year. When it is busy the deer make their way to the Sanctury. But they are not very timid. The red deer are more stand-offish.

The jackdaws were making a thorough job of mobbing something, what it was I don't know but I have heard it several times up in tall trees and not seen it fly out. It has a voice which I could imagine belongs to a sparrow-hawk; an alarmed high-pitched 'ki-ki ki ki ki.' In this case they were in stereo and of slightly different pitch.

Granulated, like bright green cauliflower in close-up.

I thought I had got green paint on the black gloves that I am working in. No, it was this powdery Pleuro-coccus algae which grows on the enormous roots of the oak which I was sitting on.

Charnwood Forest
Leicestershire March

The quarry is 190 feet deep and is used for diving practice. Moorhens climb the 45° slopes from the water.

The hard Pre-Cambrian rocks of Charnwood are amongst the oldest in England. They underlie the softer, younger rocks of the midlands but it is only here that they appear at the surface and form craggy hills.

Pre-Cambrian siltstone has been compressed during earth-movements. Under pressure the flakey crystals of mica have lined-up in one direction. The rock splits regularly where there are sheets of mica crystals. Slates were quarried here at Swithland Great Pit during the last century. The best slate was in a bed only 15 feet wide and nearly vertical.

This moss grew on the rubbly slopes of the quarry. Some of the older shoots had what looked like red buds at the end. Cushions of the moss had been uprooted, perhaps by frost-action. Pohlia nutans is often found on old industrial sites.

At the edge of the wood, a brimstone— butter yellow. Rapid flight in March sunshine. A brown chafer beetle landed on my map.

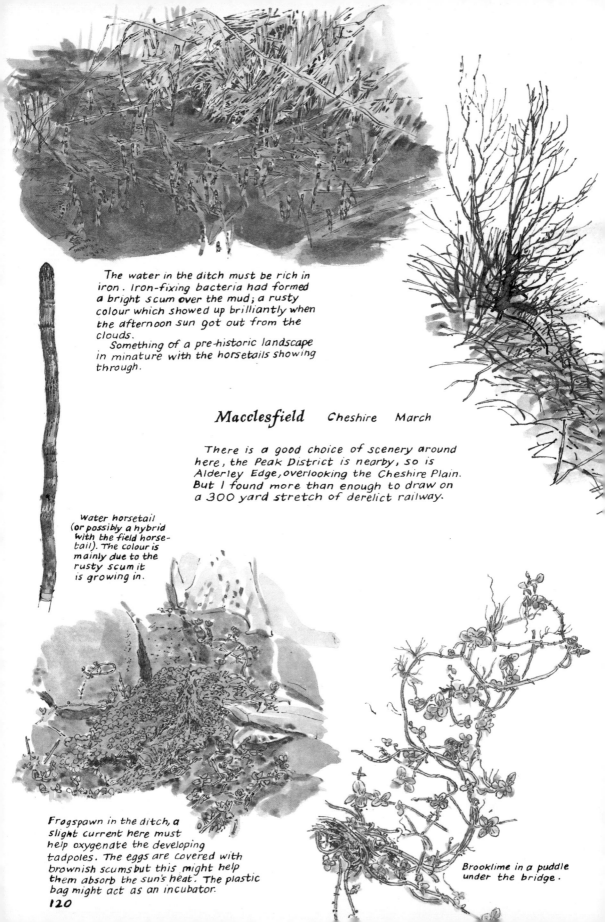

The water in the ditch must be rich in iron. Iron-fixing bacteria had formed a bright scum over the mud; a rusty colour which showed up brilliantly when the afternoon sun got out from the clouds.

Something of a pre-historic landscape in miniature with the horsetails showing through.

Macclesfield   Cheshire   March

There is a good choice of scenery around here, the Peak District is nearby, so is Alderley Edge, overlooking the Cheshire Plain. But I found more than enough to draw on a 300 yard stretch of derelict railway.

Water horsetail (or possibly a hybrid with the field horsetail). The colour is mainly due to the rusty scum it is growing in.

Frogspawn in the ditch, a slight current here must help oxygenate the developing tadpoles. The eggs are covered with brownish scums but this might help them absorb the sun's heat. The plastic bag might act as an incubator.

Brooklime in a puddle under the bridge.

120

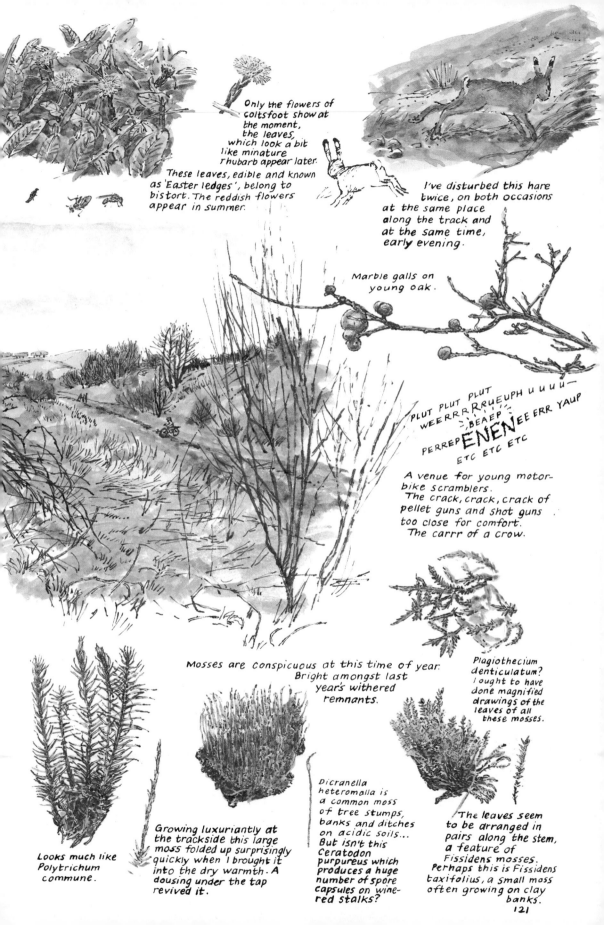

Only the flowers of coltsfoot show at the moment, the leaves, which look a bit like miniature rhubarb appear later. These leaves, edible and known as 'Easter ledges', belong to bistort. The reddish flowers appear in summer.

I've disturbed this hare twice, on both occasions at the same place along the track and at the same time, early evening.

Marble galls on young oak.

PLUT PLUT PLUT
WEERRRRRUEUPH uuuu—
PERREP BEAEP ENENEE ERR YAUP
ETC ETC ETC

A venue for young motor-bike scramblers. The crack, crack, crack of pellet guns and shot guns too close for comfort. The carrr of a crow.

Plagiothecium denticulatum? I ought to have done magnified drawings of the leaves of all these mosses.

Mosses are conspicuous at this time of year. Bright amongst last year's withered remnants.

Looks much like Polytrichum commune.

Growing luxuriantly at the trackside this large moss folded up surprisingly quickly when I brought it into the dry warmth. A dousing under the tap revived it.

Dicranella heteromalla is a common moss of tree stumps, banks and ditches on acidic soils... But isn't this Ceratodon purpureus which produces a huge number of spore capsules on wine-red stalks?

The leaves seem to be arranged in pairs along the stem, a feature of Fissidens mosses. Perhaps this is Fissidens taxifolius, a small moss often growing on clay banks.

121

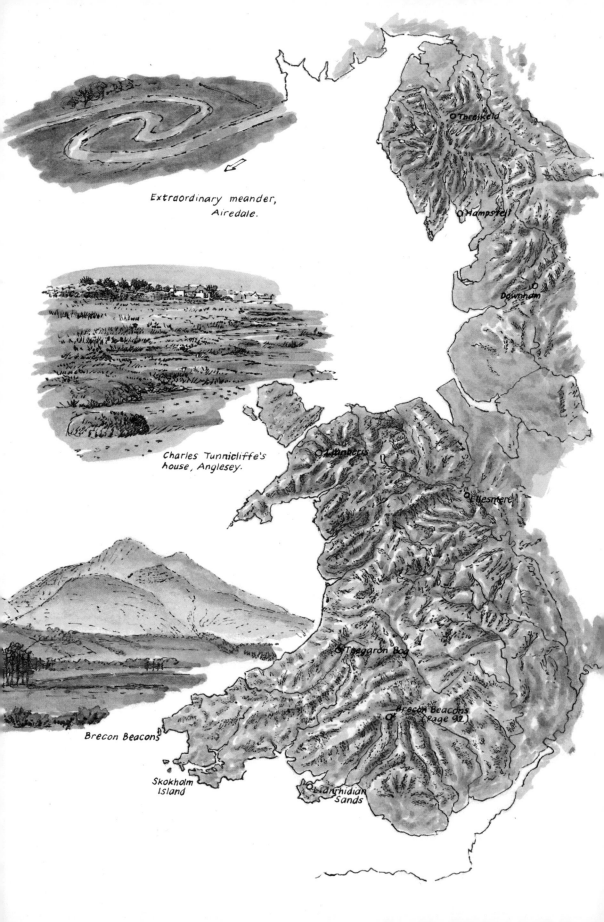

Extraordinary meander,
Airedale.

Charles Tunnicliffe's
house, Anglesey.

Brecon Beacons

Skokholm
Island

Llanrhidian
Sands

Threlkeld

Hampsfell

Downham

Llanberis

Ellesmere

Tregaron Bog

Brecon Beacons
(page 92)

WALES AND THE NORTHWEST

April–May

Life moves at a different pace in the remoter parts of Wales. On Skokholm island the weekly boat was two days late because of gales and fog, but a couple of extra days there seemed perfectly reasonable – I felt far removed from rigid timetables and busy schedules. At home I begin to worry if a bus is ten minutes late.

Back on the mainland I discovered that buses to the nearest town were infrequent and there were none at all that afternoon. Instead I got a ride on a local school bus, hitched a lift with some English holidaymakers and a large white dog, took the train from Milford Haven to Gowerton and finally caught a bus to Llanrhidian. When I arrived there late in the evening it took me two hours to find a bed and breakfast – I eventually had to walk to the next village.

Across the Burry inlet from Llanrhidian I could see the glimmering lights of Llanelli on the Welsh coalfield. The massive steelworks there is now suffering the effects of the world recession, yet on the Gower side of the peninsula it sometimes seems as if little has changed since the Middle Ages. As the tide ebbed next morning to reveal a vast expanse of saltmarsh, mud flats and sandbanks, a procession of horse-drawn carts set out across the estuary to gather cockles. When the Industrial Revolution brought roads and railways to south Wales the market for these shellfish increased enormously, to the extent that a few years ago there were hardly any cockles left to gather. The harvesting had to stop for a while, although perhaps not surprisingly the authorities put the blame for this on birds rather than men. Oystercatchers were named as the chief culprits and thousands were shot, many of them European birds that only wintered in Britain. But some local people believe that exploitation by humans was the real cause of the decline in cockle numbers.

I journeyed northwards through Wales by bus, eventually arriving at Llanberis in Snowdonia. This may be a time-consuming form of travel but it is an excellent way to see the countryside; in wilder areas the road has to wind around the scenery. As I'm so tall I generally have a cramped view out of a car and, besides, if I was driving along the narrow roads of Wales I wouldn't have much time to gaze at hills. This is one of those areas where people overtake just before a dangerous bend or an unexpected humpback bridge. Anyway, there was a great deal to see on this journey. At Carmarthen we passed the blackened remains of an oak, the subject of Merlin's prophecy which is, I believe, 'When the tree falls down so shall the town.' An old superstition, but the people of Carmarthen aren't taking any chances; the tree is held up and heavily restored with concrete.

Much of central Wales is high plateau, eaten into by narrow steep-sided valleys. But the bus did come down into one fairly wide valley where the university town of Lampeter lies surrounded by trees and pastures. There is an Iron Age hill fort near by. I broke my journey here for a night, and in the twilight that evening I took a walk along the meadows on the outskirts of the town by the River Teifi. From the bridge I could hear someone playing a balalaika; several students were reclining on the bank of the river. Lampeter, I had been told, has a strange effect on students. I can believe it. The greenery and the balmy air make it a restful place.

I also stopped off at Tregaron to see the bog there which stretches for miles between the hills. In order to get a proper view of it I walked out of the village and then climbed up through a wood of moss-covered oaks and beeches until I reached open hillside. Larks were rising and a pair of ravens flew, honking, back and forth across the vast brown expanse of the bog. From the hills on the other side, which must have been a good five miles away, I could hear a dog barking.

In England I am used to travelling the 180 miles from Yorkshire to London in just two hours by train. In Wales, however, it took me twelve hours to get from Tregaron to Llanberis – half the distance, and I had to change buses four times. But then in Wales the bus seems to be more of a social service than a rapid transit system. The driver stopped at isolated cottages to drop off parcels, and as we went through straggling villages and winding lanes we picked up passengers wherever they flagged the bus down. Old people with weatherbeaten faces lugged huge loads on board, then settled back in their seats and chatted in Welsh.

But railways are still my favourite form of travel. It is easier to draw on a train than on a bus and a rail journey gives extra clues to the landscape; every so often a cutting slices neatly through a hillside to reveal the nature of the underlying rock. In north Wales, where the line follows the narrow strip of level ground between the mountains and the sea, the rocks have been buckled to form a huge dome – the result of a collision between drifting continents some 400 million years ago. The structure is similar to that of the Weald of Kent and Surrey, but it is on a much grander scale.

Although the upfolded rocks have been eroded away, you can still get some idea of the size of these geological changes when you realise that both Snowdon and Cader Idris were originally in *down*folds along the rim of this dome.

In the early stages of this continental collision volcanoes poured vast quantities of lava and ash into the sea. These craggy slopes of volcanic rock contrast with the smoother, greener hills of slate in Snowdonia; slate is formed when muddy sediments are folded under heat and pressure deep within the Earth. In the cliffs of Skokholm it is easy to see how red sandstone has been folded. On the north side of the island at Mad Bay the rock layers lean outwards over the sea and provide inaccessible ledges on which razorbills, guillemots and fulmars nest. But at Crab Bay, on the south side, the layers lean inland and provide slopes where puffins nest in rabbit holes.

Slate quarrying is the only major industry that north Wales has ever had. Llanberis, for instance, is dominated by the remains of a huge quarry. The history of this industry in Wales is one of ruthless exploitation comparable to the worst excesses of the mill tyrants and mine owners of nineteenth-century England. Many slate-quarry workers succumbed to pneumoconiosis, the disease caused by dust particles that also affects coalminers. But now most quarries are derelict. When I was in Llanberis a hydro-electric plant was being constructed inside the mountain where the slate used to be worked, and the quarry buildings housed a museum.

After I had been to Wales I visited the Lake District. This too is an often rugged area with a wide diversity of scenery, but on a more intimate scale. The Lake District is ideal for walking in. The hills here have been likened to the spokes of a cartwheel, with valleys and lakes in the spaces between. And the different sorts of rock form scenery of different character. On the southern edge of the area I drew limestone pavement on Hampsfell, while at Threlkeld slate gives Saddleback a smoother outline. Around Windermere the country that lies on ancient Silurian rocks is lush and well wooded – a softer side to lakeland scenery.

While I was at Windermere I went to see Beatrix Potter's house at Sawrey. On reaching the village I felt as though I knew the place already, so much does it resemble the watercolours that illustrate Peter Rabbit, Mrs Tiggy-Winkle and Pigling Bland. At the house itself you can see the staircase that appears in Samuel Whiskers, a doll's house containing the pottery food stolen by Hunca Munca and Tom Thumb in *The Tale of Two Bad Mice*, even the rhubarb patch favoured by Jemima Puddleduck. I also called at Ambleside library to look at some of Beatrix Potter's meticulous studies of fungi. Incredibly, the botanists at Kew Gardens thought her work wasn't scientific enough when she showed them some of her drawings. Perhaps it is just as well that she was unable to make a career of botany. If she had become a professional scientific illustrator we might never have seen the animal stories.

Unusually wide range of media for me; pen & ink,
bamboo pen, watercolour, a bit of guoache and a
gull-dropping.

126

MAD BAY, SKOKHOLM ISLAND.
April

I've never seen anything like the fog that has just come in. Only 15 minutes ago I noticed clouds of what I thought was spray moving up the hollows between the cliffs, now even the nearest cliff is a silhouette. There's been not a cloud in the sky all day and there is a breeze— but the breeze is actually blowing the wall of fog towards the shore.

Ground ivy.

127

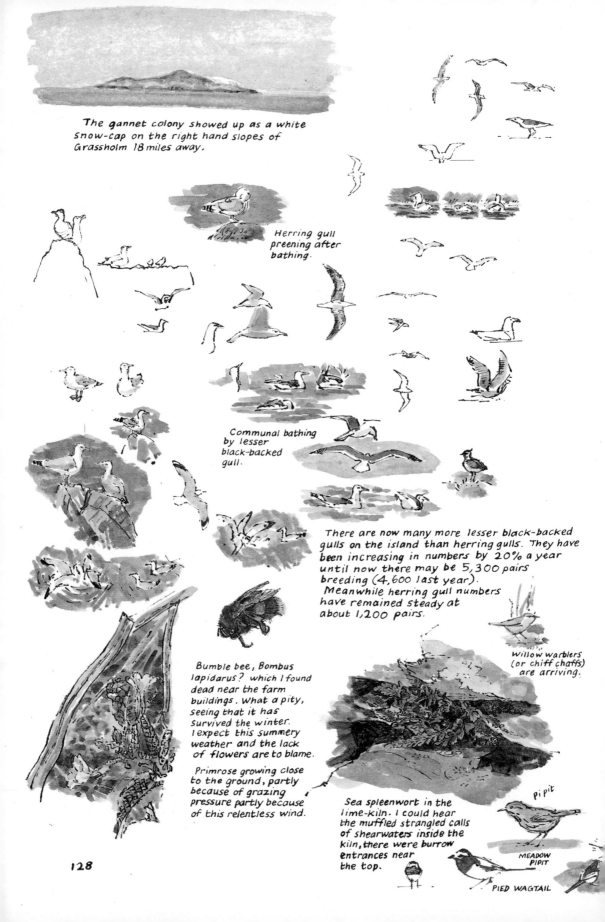

The gannet colony showed up as a white snow-cap on the right hand slopes of Grassholm 18 miles away.

Herring gull preening after bathing.

Communal bathing by lesser black-backed gull.

There are now many more lesser black-backed gulls on the island than herring gulls. They have been increasing in numbers by 20% a year until now there may be 5,300 pairs breeding (4,600 last year). Meanwhile herring gull numbers have remained steady at about 1,200 pairs.

Willow warblers (or chiff chaffs) are arriving.

Bumble bee, Bombus lapidarus? which I found dead near the farm buildings. What a pity, seeing that it has survived the winter. I expect this summery weather and the lack of flowers are to blame.

Primrose growing close to the ground, partly because of grazing pressure partly because of this relentless wind.

Sea spleenwort in the lime-kiln. I could hear the muffled strangled calls of shearwaters inside the kiln, there were burrow entrances near the top.

pipit

MEADOW PIPIT

PIED WAGTAIL

A cormorant struggled to swallow a fish. A couple of minutes later it is still making swallowing movements.

After 5 or 10 minutes it resumed a classic cormorant shape.

100 or so gulls mobbing a buzzard.

pip pa rip
par rip pa rip
pa rip

Oystercatchers

Common limpet

Plumaria elegans, a small red seaweed.

Limpet with fledgling seaweed decorating its shell.

Lecanora atra, Black shields lichen, grows on rocks near the sea ... I don't know if this is it. Black shield lichen is shown as even more rough and warted than this in books.

Skokholm island is extremely rich in lichens, every rock has 3 or 4 species growing on it.

129

Thursday 10th April
In excess of 31 razorbills
in Crab Bay, which I soon
noticed were in pairs.

A _swallow_
for the log

Cormorant

Flapping display..

..circling..

.. they seem to
be preening each
other under the
chin, or bill-tapping

They open their bills but
there's no noise I can hear,
unless it is a slight hoarse
creaking croak.
All I hear is
the patter of
ripples as one
takes off.

A honey bee settled on
my watch, preened for a
moment then investigated
the top of my water bottle.
The first insect of the
season to be caught out
in this way. I must have
confused hundreds of
hoverflies with the same
trick last Summer.

The puffin's voice is like
a softly distant complaining
chain-saw.. wooeerr
oooaurrr

Wheatear
disappearing
into a burrow
with a grass
stem.

Grey
seal

This drawing might
have been more
finished but the
puffins were enjoying
the evening sun,
standing in pairs
outside their burrows,
when I came
back from a
tea-break so I
decided to leave
them in peace.

I looked to see what the cloud of smoke was. Through binoculars I could see a boiling of white specks in the wake of the ship.

It seemed a long way out to be gulls following the ship. Perhaps they were terns or even gannets.

Gnats or mosquitos dancing before my eyes.

Plastic icon which must have been carried 2 or 3 miles from the mainland by a gull. An appropriate decoration for a lesser black-backed gull's nest.

Carol the warden once found quite a large doll with an arm missing in a pool in the gull colony. She wondered what the arm sticking up out of the water could be.

White wagtail; note that the black cap and bib do not join up.

pipit!

Mutant rabbit chasing one of its fellows. The island has far more colour variants amongst its rabbits than a mainland population. As the rabbit numbers on the island vary from 10,000 in a good summer to 200 in a bad winter it's not surprising that odd things happen geneticly. Even so out of 100 rabbits 99 are the normal grey brown.

In the drawing of Crab Bay opposite the tarry darkness on the lower rocks is the zone of black lichens. These are crust-like lichens which can withstand the buffeting of high tide. In the orange zone above, which is subject to sea-spray, yellow leaf-like lichens are able to survive. But the bright red between the black and yellow is the rock itself, old red sandstone, the layers are tilted at 45°.

Ripple-marked piece of Old red sandstone embedded in the track near the buildings. It showed up particularly well in the evening sunlight.

131

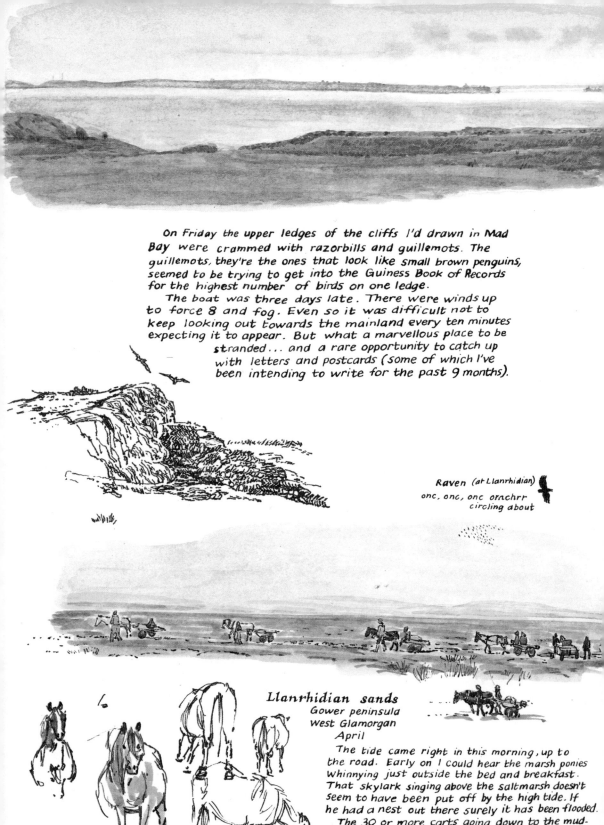

On Friday the upper ledges of the cliffs I'd drawn in Mad Bay were crammed with razorbills and guillemots. The guillemots, they're the ones that look like small brown penguins, seemed to be trying to get into the Guiness Book of Records for the highest number of birds on one ledge.

The boat was three days late. There were winds up to force 8 and fog. Even so it was difficult not to keep looking out towards the mainland every ten minutes expecting it to appear. But what a marvellous place to be stranded... and a rare opportunity to catch up with letters and postcards (some of which I've been intending to write for the past 9 months).

Raven (at Llanrhidian)
onc, onc, onc ornchrr
circling about

Llanrhidian sands
Gower peninsula
West Glamorgan
April

The tide came right in this morning, up to the road. Early on I could hear the marsh ponies whinnying just outside the bed and breakfast. That skylark singing above the saltmarsh doesn't seem to have been put off by the high tide. If he had a nest out there surely it has been flooded.

The 30 or more carts going down to the mud-flats for cockles are the sort of incident I'd expect to find Turner sketching. The bright colours make it look like a medieval baggage wagon trek or a Canterbury pilgrimage or King John's luggage crossing the Wash.

132

WRONG!
That'll teach you not to think about travel arrangements & worry about noisy motor-bikes when you should be concentrating on drawing.

There are curlew, oystercatchers and redshanks on the marsh, goodness knows what in the hedges. I wish I knew the voices of half these birds. That distinctive echoing ring like a hammer striking metal.

Oh, it is a hammer, in the nearby lorry yard.

I was right first time, it was a bird—a raven. Unless the chap with the hammer can run 50 yards in 10 seconds.

Gorse

At the foot of the gorse bush, on a pony dropping, a pair of spiders in courtship ritual. The male approaching the female waving his forelegs in semaphore.

Lesser sharp sea rush, Juncus maritimus, on the roadside bank on the edge of the saltmarsh.

An attempt to make a detailed study of a violet was foiled when a stream of mini-buses full of field studiers began pouring along the narrow hedge-banked lane.

133

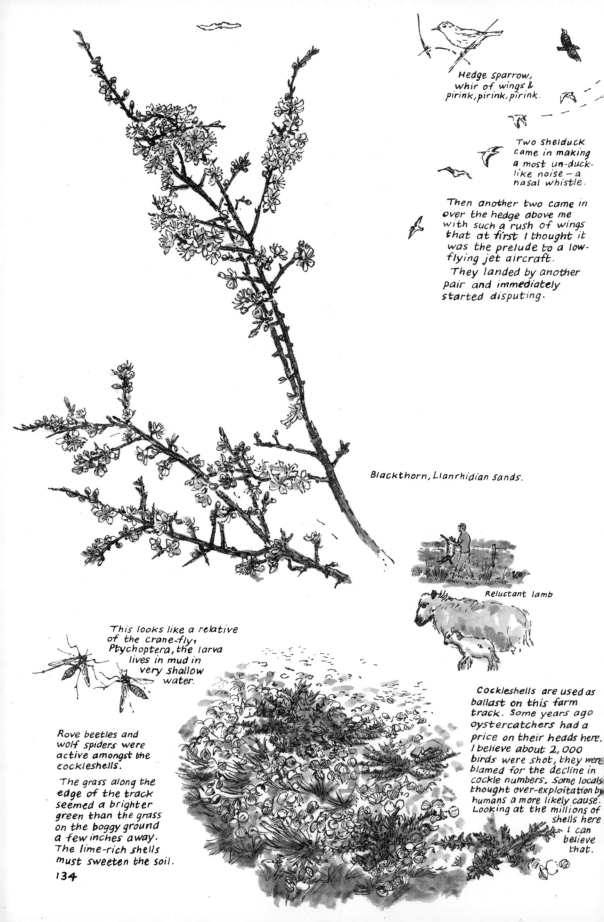

Hedge sparrow,
whir of wings &
pirink, pirink, pirink.

Two shelduck
came in making
a most un-duck-
like noise — a
nasal whistle.

Then another two came in
over the hedge above me
with such a rush of wings
that at first I thought it
was the prelude to a low-
flying jet aircraft.
  They landed by another
pair and immediately
started disputing.

Blackthorn, Llanrhidian sands.

Reluctant lamb

This looks like a relative
of the crane-fly,
Ptychoptera, the larva
lives in mud in
very shallow
water.

Rove beetles and
wolf spiders were
active amongst the
cockleshells.

  The grass along the
edge of the track
seemed a brighter
green than the grass
on the boggy ground
a few inches away.
The lime-rich shells
must sweeten the soil.

Cockleshells are used as
ballast on this farm
track. Some years ago
oystercatchers had a
price on their heads here.
I believe about 2,000
birds were shot, they were
blamed for the decline in
cockle numbers. Some locals
thought over-exploitation by
humans a more likely cause.
Looking at the millions of
            shells here
             I can
             believe
             that.

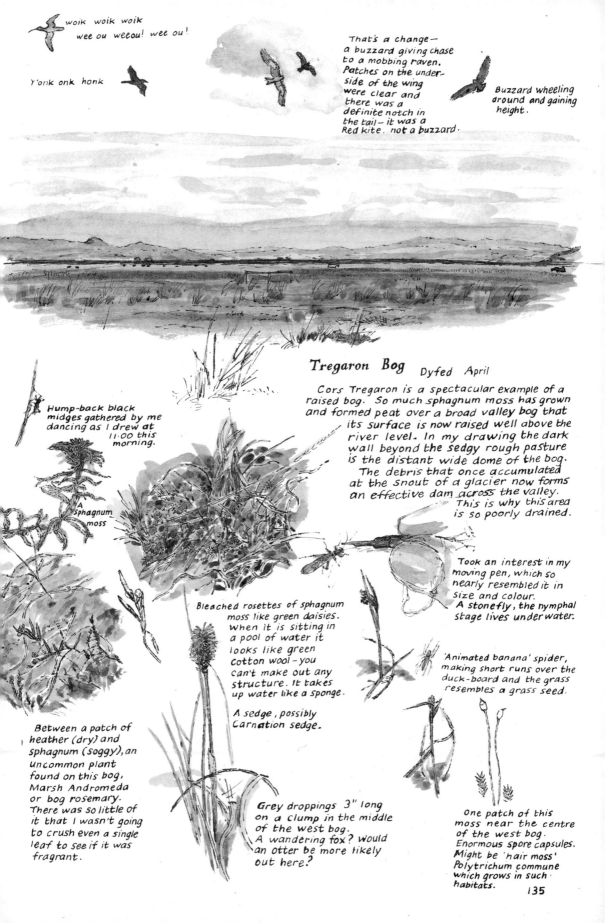

woik woik woik
wee ou weeou! wee ou!

Y'onk onk honk

That's a change—
a buzzard giving chase
to a mobbing raven.
Patches on the under-
side of the wing
were clear and
there was a
definite notch in
the tail—it was a
Red kite, not a buzzard.

Buzzard wheeling
around and gaining
height.

Tregaron Bog Dyfed April

Cors Tregaron is a spectacular example of a
raised bog. So much sphagnum moss has grown
and formed peat over a broad valley bog that
its surface is now raised well above the
river level. In my drawing the dark
wall beyond the sedgy rough pasture
is the distant wide dome of the bog.
The debris that once accumulated
at the snout of a glacier now forms
an effective dam across the valley.
This is why this area
is so poorly drained.

Hump-back black
midges gathered by me
dancing as I drew at
11:00 this
morning.

A
Sphagnum
moss

Took an interest in my
moving pen, which so
nearly resembled it in
size and colour.
A stonefly, the nymphal
stage lives under water.

Bleached rosettes of sphagnum
moss like green daisies.
When it is sitting in
a pool of water it
looks like green
cotton wool—you
can't make out any
structure. It takes
up water like a sponge.

A sedge, possibly
Carnation sedge.

'Animated banana' spider,
making short runs over the
duck-board and the grass
resembles a grass seed.

Between a patch of
heather (dry) and
sphagnum (soggy), an
uncommon plant
found on this bog,
Marsh Andromeda
or bog rosemary.
There was so little of
it that I wasn't going
to crush even a single
leaf to see if it was
fragrant.

Grey droppings 3" long
on a clump in the middle
of the west bog.
A wandering fox? Would
an otter be more likely
out here?

One patch of this
moss near the centre
of the west bog.
Enormous spore capsules.
Might be 'hair moss'
Polytrichum commune
which grows in such
habitats.

135

Llanberis Gwynedd April

For once I felt I had to draw the classic postcard view. It's unbeatable. The peak of Snowdon is hidden to the right, but this is appropriate; it is the effect of the moods of the air on the hills and the way this is reflected to a varying extent in the water that make this view; it is different each time you look at it.

That must be my first cuckoo!

I put up a Common Sandpiper from the lakeside, it took off with a stiff-winged fluttery flight.

Spur notched

A smaller than usual water crowfoot, the moorland crowfoot, Ranunculus omiophyllus, in shallow water on a boggy, peaty patch on the hillside.

Common Dog violet. At Llanrhidian sands a burst of traffic had prevented me properly drawing a hedgerow violet. Here I was surprised by a train passing by along the lakeside railway. Mmmm... the grimy smell of steam, takes me back to school days, the school overlooked the marshalling yards.

Willow warbler, musical ascending and descending song, tailing off wistfully. 3-4 seconds long about once every 10 seconds.

Wood sorrel growing on an ash trunk overhanging a stream, the trunk covered with polypody ferns, ivy and moss.

Resembling burnt toast on the underside: an aged specimen

Birch bracket fungus, Piptoporus betulinus. The old birch trunk also supported ivy, lichen and mosses.

This rock is called Craig yr Undeb, the Union rock. It looks to me as if it has been polished smooth by glaciers coming down the valley.

137

Canada goose

Mallards in the evening
coming ashore

Goldfinches
chinking, tinkling across

Territorial disputes
among the
blackbirds

Birds in Tricia's playground
from a park shelter in soft
April rain. Just the day
for drawing from the Boat
house Café.

Brood of nine ducklings.

Heron and the inevitable mobbing crow.

The Mere
Ellesmere
Shropshire
April

Coots

Gosling, three of them

Poorly looking black-headed gull.

The hens appeared one day and adopted the café as their home.

Kitten preparing to enter through broken pane in door. An orphan; thinks Henrietta is its mum.

The meres have scarcely any inflow and outflow. So they can't be called lakes, they're more like huge puddles. Blocks of ice embedded in glacial debris left holes where they melted.

Downham
Lancashire May

Pendle hill isn't normally this colour—it was doing
its Ayers Rock trick, glowing in the late sunlight(8·00
−8·30 PM). Glowing more effectively than I can show.

All day white smoke billowed downwards from the
middle part of the hill. Burning off old heather, I
should think.

I thought I was lucky to have a
fly keep still for so long. Then I
noticed the bodies of two more
flies on the lower twig. Was it
a spider that had
got them, there
were no webs
nearby.
Perhaps they
were victims
of a parasitic
fungus.

Chinese character
moth, or some-
thing similar,
at rest in
the hedge.

Water avens with lesser
celandine and goosegrass
at the foot of the hedge.

Two bees in frantic
tussle on a dandelion.

Like miniature *forced rhubarb. I think these bright red seedlings are sycamore, they were under one of the enormous mature sycamores which thrive round here.*

A sound as if Worser hill was cracking open and a jet went over about 50 feet above my head. A curlew got up calling.

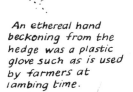

Could be Mesembrina meridiana, the larva feeds on horse or cattle-dung.

An ethereal hand beckoning from the hedge was a plastic glove such as is used by farmers at lambing time.

chak! Chaumm!

25-plus jackdaws got up off the turf of the hill and the heron changed course.

Primrose on shady bank by a stream.

This is perfect country for walking; you soon get somewhere. There are hedges, woods and streams, you go down into a dip then climb up past ashes, thorns and gorse to open hillside with limestone walls. The view is constantly changing, opening out to something fresh.

Only after a day or so did I realise that something was missing. There are no pylons or even telegraph poles, no advertisement hoardings or illuminated signs. Even the phone box in the village is grey to tone in with the local stonework.

Rusty stain on limestone gatepost loaded with fossil sea lily stems.

141

I didn't notice any fossils in the weathered lichen-covered limestone pavement. But on my way back from an extended lunch-break in Cartmel, as I stooped down to see if a sun-bathing lamb was injured, I noticed many of the rocks in the drystone wall contained fossils. One stone was entirely made up of coral. Growing packed together in a colony like this the polyps lived in polygonal cases. Fossil coral in adjacent rocks which had grown in isolation was oval.

Bracken growing from beneath a boulder. The boulder is evidently of different material than the limestone bedrock. Parts of it are polished black. The lichens growing on it are different to those which grow on the limestone. The whole rock has a greenish cast and it is more angular and layered than the weathered chunks of limestone pavement.

It is an erratic boulder, a Silurian rock brought here to rest on the less ancient Carboniferous limestone by a glacier during the Ice Age.

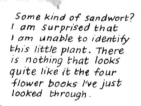

Some kind of sandwort? I am surprised that I am unable to identify this little plant. There is nothing that looks quite like it the four flower books I've just looked through.

A sedge going to seed?

Field Woodrush

Common violet on the hillside. Tooth white. The leaves seem to have furled themselves to resist this desiccating wind.

Half the size of an average butterfly the green was iridescent, not such a bad match for the young hawthorn leaves.

It was a green hairstreak, when it opens its wings the upper surface is brown.

Hampsfell *Cumbria   May*

Around the Hospice on the top of the fell the exposed limestone has been weathered to form pavement. The cracks and joints and sculptured surfaces are formed where rain has dissolved away the rock.

This limestone was laid down in a tropical sea over 300 million years ago, hence the coral. At this time the continental plates of North America and Europe were drifting together. About 150 million years later when the two plates were splitting apart along the line of the Atlantic much of England was again swamped by a warm shallow sea. I drew the Jurassic limestone that formed in this later sea along its outcrop at Lincoln Edge and in the Cotswolds as well as at its tail-end, Portland Bill.

143

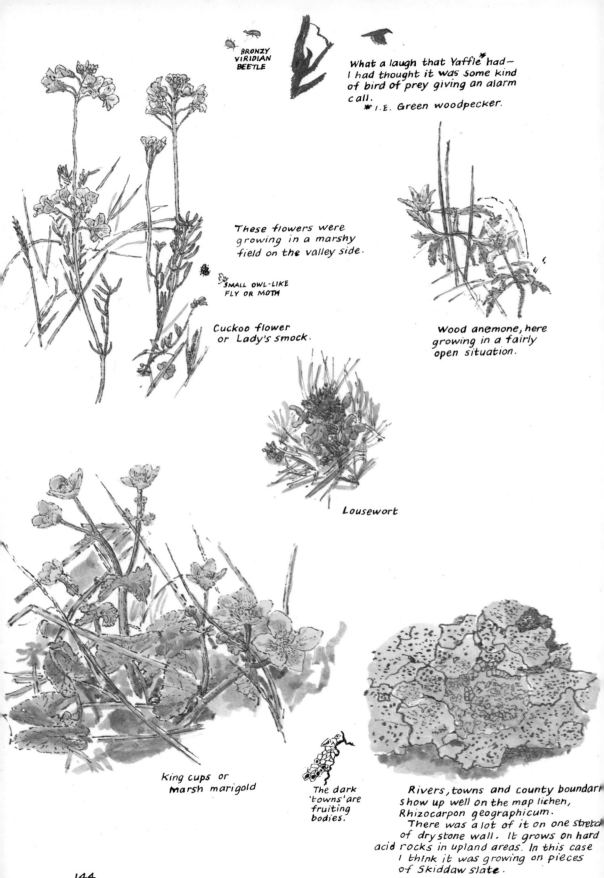

BRONZY
VIRIDIAN
BEETLE

What a laugh that Yaffle* had—
I had thought it was some kind
of bird of prey giving an alarm
call.
* I.E. Green woodpecker.

These flowers were
growing in a marshy
field on the valley side.

SMALL OWL-LIKE
FLY OR MOTH

Cuckoo flower
or Lady's smock.

Wood anemone, here
growing in a fairly
open situation.

Lousewort

King cups or
Marsh marigold

The dark
'towns' are
fruiting
bodies.

Rivers, towns and county boundar[i]
show up well on the map lichen,
Rhizocarpon geographicum.
There was a lot of it on one stretc[h]
of dry stone wall. It grows on hard
acid rocks in upland areas. In this case
I think it was growing on pieces
of Skiddaw slate.

Threlkeld   Cumbria   May

I saw a swallow flying into the barn.
The hill is Saddleback or Blencathra.

Until I looked closely I thought
the flowers of bilberry were
red berries.

I think this largish caterpillar
is that of the northern eggar,
the upland form of the oak
eggar moth. Often it will feed
on heather but it will tackle a
variety of low-growing foodplants
and this one was on the bilberry.

This individual will have over-
wintered as a caterpillar. It will
munch its way through the summer,
spend the winter as a chrysalis and
emerge as an adult moth next
summer.

A case of mistaken identity,
first one sheep, then four,
then thirty-five from all
quarters of the field converged
on me baa-ing after me.
That number of sheep make
a lot of noise, it was quite
alarming having them trotting
five-a-breast behind me.
The sheep on the other side
of the fence joined in too.

Later I saw the shepherd,
his tweeds were just the
same colour of green as my
anorak and trousers, and
he had a bag over his
shoulder.

When I returned through
the field it was warmer, I'd
taken off my anorak and
put it in my haversack. The
sheep took no notice of me.

Suilven

Balivanich
Benbecula

Sands of Forvie

Lochboisdale,
South
Uist

Loch Garten

Pass of Killiecrankie

Rannoch
Moor

Pencaitland

Gourock

Berwick

Peebles

Castle
Douglas

Corbridge

Terrington

Beech trees on drumlins
near Castle Douglas.

LAIRIG GHRU

The Cairngorms from Aviemore station.

SCOTLAND AND NORTHUMBRIA

May – July

Amongst the mountains and glens of Scotland you can still find plants, birds and animals that colonised our island as the ice-sheets retreated. In the Outer Hebrides and along the northwest coast there are rocks more ancient than any found in England and Wales. Scotland, in fact, was originally part of the North American continent; an accident of continental drift welded it to England about 400 million years ago. Even its people are different. The remoteness of the country and the difficulties of making a living from this harsh land have produced tightly knit communities with their own traditions and cultures.

The landscape of the Scottish Borders, however, is gentler than the rocky country to the north. Abbeys and mellow towns nestle quietly in broad green valleys, with wide views of rivers winding down from distant hills. There is an air of sturdy prosperity here, but it has been hard won. Castles and fortified houses stand guard over strategic points, reminders of the troubled history of the region for so long contested by English and Scottish kings. It is an almost biblical landscape, where an atmosphere of religious fervour, an independent puritanism, still lingers.

In Scotland my plan of a more or less clockwise journey around Britain finally came to grief. There are too many fjords to allow easy travel up the west coast. Indeed, the forces that have shaped the Highlands are everywhere dramatically in evidence. Edinburgh is dominated by the remains of a volcano which was active 300 million years ago. North of Glasgow railways and roads make their way below stark peaks shattered by frost action and along lochs that have flooded ice-deepened valleys. So the main route to the central Highlands is by road and rail via the gorge of Killiecrankie, through the high Pass of Drumochter and down across Speyside.

I headed north with the intention of staying in Pitlochry, but this was far busier than I remembered it from childhood holidays and after a brief look around I decided to go on to Killiecrankie. This proved to be an excellent base from which to explore the surrounding country and find interesting subjects to draw. There is a nature trail near by, and on the advice of the Visitor Centre I set off along it to get some background on the local wildlife. The trail guide had evidently been written by a keen forester – everything was described from the point of view of a tree. Deer nibbled the tops off saplings while squirrels stripped bark and blackcock fed on the young buds. Even when full grown, the trees are still affected by squirrels and crossbills taking the seeds from cones, and the turkey-sized capercaillie feeds almost exclusively on pine-needles.

I also visited Rannoch Moor, farther to the east. The railway station there, the highest in Britain, is 15 miles from the town it serves. This is harsh, desolate country. The moor stretches for miles in every direction, and one looks out over a silent, deserted landscape ringed by mountains. It can hardly have changed since the moor was a centre of ice-spreading many thousands of years ago. First the main valleys became blocked with ice and then the glaciers were forced up side valleys. Glencoe was enlarged in this way by a tongue of ice making its way from Rannoch to the Great Glen.

Away to the northeast of Rannoch lies Speyside, a place I've returned to again and again over the past ten years. I've regularly worked there as a volunteer warden on the RSPB's Loch Garten osprey reserve. Speyside has a wide range of habitats – moorland, farmland, bog, loch and pine forest. There is a varied coastline near by and the area is dominated by the Cairngorm plateau with its tundra conditions. Some stretches of the original Caledonian pine forest still survive; rough, open ground with heather, birch and bog and isolated stands of Scots pine. Forest of this sort covered most of Scotland after the ice retreated and man began to arrive.

The return of the osprey to Scotland is a classic success story of nature conservation. These eagle-like fish hunters have nested at Loch Garten since 1958, although in that year the eggs were stolen and so now a twenty-four hour watch is kept until the young are safely fledged. It is hard to believe that such birds should be threatened by egg collectors – I thought so when I worked on the reserve at Easter 1971, but a few weeks later I read that the eggs had been stolen in a night raid. Despite such setbacks, however, the ospreys have steadily increased in number and their future now seems reasonably assured.

But for me, the high point of my visit to Scotland was a week in the Outer Hebrides. It was like a journey to another world. The ferry sails from Oban on the mainland, where the water in the harbour was so clear that I could see transparent jellyfish swimming alongside the boat. Leaving the harbour, we followed the Sound of Mull, a long fjord-like channel between Mull and the mainland, past the tip of the Ardnamurchan peninsula and the island of Coll, and out across the open sea to Barra.

Here at the main town, Castlebay, a crowd was gathered at the quayside as the boat pulled in. It seemed that most of the townspeople were there, including a party of Girl Guides. We thought that perhaps the coming of the ferry was a major event, but the crowd had assembled for a quite different reason. They were waiting to receive a coffin that was on board. We waited while it was taken off and then the mourners, led by a veiled woman in black supported by two other women, followed the pallbearers up the narrow winding road from the quayside. The low evening sun brought out the texture of the rocky hillside behind the town. It could have been a Mediterranean scene, it was so different to the way things happen on the mainland. Someone on board took a photograph; it didn't seem the right thing to do.

There is one main road on South Uist which runs from the harbour at Lochboisdale northwards to Benbecula (which is joined to South Uist by a long bridge). There is no bus service, but I was able to get a lift with the postman, who was making his deliveries by van. One local Post Office was a bungalow down a side road by a small lochan. There were chickens scratching around the door and the only indication that it was a Post Office was a tiny notice fixed to the wall. Near by were three of the traditional Scottish black houses. One was used as a barn, another was derelict. This type of building was – and still is – used by crofters, with thick stone walls rounded at the corners to reduce wind resistance, a turf roof and only one door. They can be made with local materials and without much in the way of technology. They might look unsophisticated, but their insulation is more efficient than that of a modern house with its double glazing, cavity-wall filling and loft insulation. This must be an important consideration when the winters are long and you have to spend much of the summer cutting and drying peat.

I was surprised by the amount of Gaelic that was spoken. People talked and joked with the postman in Gaelic, but I never got the impression that the locals used it so we foreigners couldn't understand what they were saying, they spoke in such a natural and cheerful way. It would be a pity if such island communities, so well adapted to making a living from the land and the sea without plundering natural resources, were to die away. But life is difficult. On Benbecula farming is confined to a narrow strip along the west coast, though sheep graze much of the island. The economy is now very dependent on the army, which has a gunnery range on South Uist.

This was my first visit to the Outer Hebrides and northwest Scotland. I felt I was journeying into the heart of an extraordinary and remote wilderness. Landscapes are like friends; the more you get to know them the more you care about them. I like to get to know somewhere in all its moods and seasons. Benbecula and Suilven already mean a lot to me, although I'll probably only ever feel really at home in the more familiar territory of the north of England. We can't all live in the wilderness, but in an increasingly ordered society it is reassuring to know that it still exists.

Common birdsfoot trefoil growing on the dunes.

I think this is Candidula intersecta, the wrinkled snail, of 'dry and open sites especially dunes and grassland,' according to the Field Guide to Land Snails.

Ribwort plantain

Cormorants

Great northern diver, diving in the bay.

On the beach a sparrow was picking the downy white feathers from the breast of a herring gull lying dead on the strand line.

The eiders are so bouyant that it takes some effort to dive under.

Fulmar

♂ Eider

♀ seemed to have a shell which she was swinging about in her bill.

Seaside pansy grows on dunes of the north and west, also on the sandy heaths of East Anglia.

Could this be the seaweed known as Carragheen or Irish moss?

SPIRORBIS WORMS

SEA MAT

150

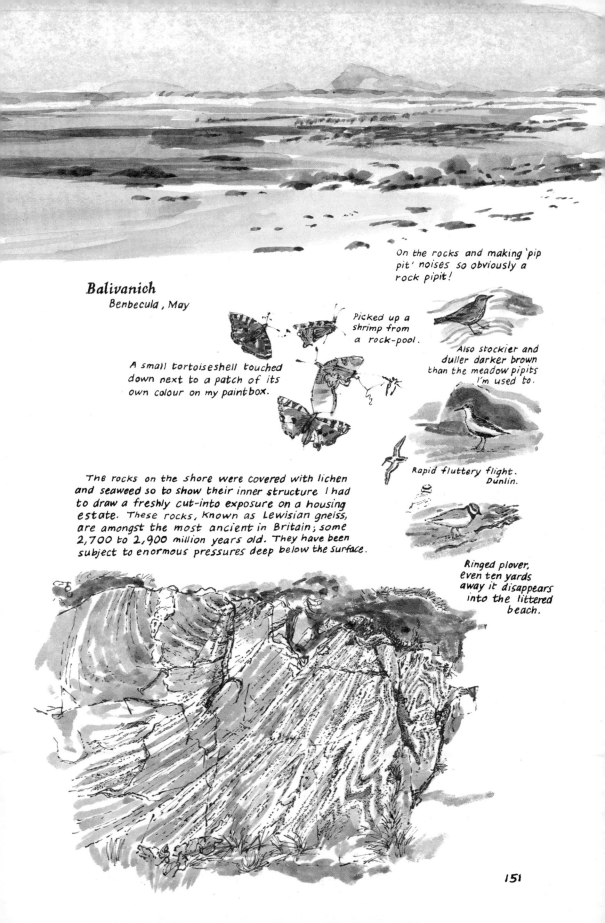

On the rocks and making 'pip pit' noises so obviously a rock pipit!

Balivanich
Benbecula, May

Picked up a shrimp from a rock-pool.

A small tortoiseshell touched down next to a patch of its own colour on my paintbox.

Also stockier and duller darker brown than the meadow pipits I'm used to.

The rocks on the shore were covered with lichen and seaweed so to show their inner structure I had to draw a freshly cut-into exposure on a housing estate. These rocks, known as Lewisian gneiss, are amongst the most ancient in Britain; some 2,700 to 2,900 million years old. They have been subject to enormous pressures deep below the surface.

Rapid fluttery flight.
Dunlin.

Ringed plover, even ten yards away it disappears into the littered beach.

REDSHANK

OYSTERCATCHER

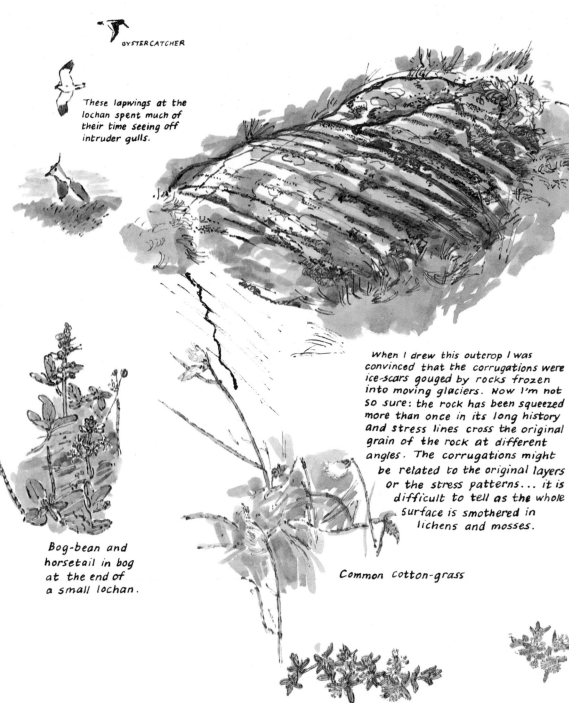

These lapwings at the lochan spent much of their time seeing off intruder gulls.

When I drew this outcrop I was convinced that the corrugations were ice-scars gouged by rocks frozen into moving glaciers. Now I'm not so sure: the rock has been squeezed more than once in its long history and stress lines cross the original grain of the rock at different angles. The corrugations might be related to the original layers or the stress patterns... it is difficult to tell as the whole surface is smothered in lichens and mosses.

Bog-bean and horsetail in bog at the end of a small lochan.

Common cotton-grass

The leaves remind me of thyme or rockrose but the small flowers don't seem to have any petals.

View across a sea-loch at Lochboisdale, you can tell that it is tidal by the zone of black lichen above the waterline. It is easier to give an impression of the South Uist landscape in a drawing than it was on the more horizontal terrain of Benbecula.

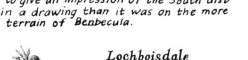

Lochboisdale
South Uist, May

Spider with appropriate thistle motif on its abdomen.

Broad surfaces for the attachment of leg muscles.

I found a swan skeleton in a roadside ditch below telephone wires. A large structure but extremely light compared with sheep bones. This piece is the hip-girdle, the vertebrae are fused together for strength, the legs are under enormous pressure during touch-down. A swan has 25 vertebrae in its neck, 18 more than a giraffe.

Thrift, here growing right on the strand line.

Eigg from the ferry; the volcanic pitchstone of An Sgùrr forms the dramatic cliff. Is that Muck or Ardnamurchan in the foreground?

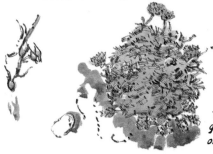

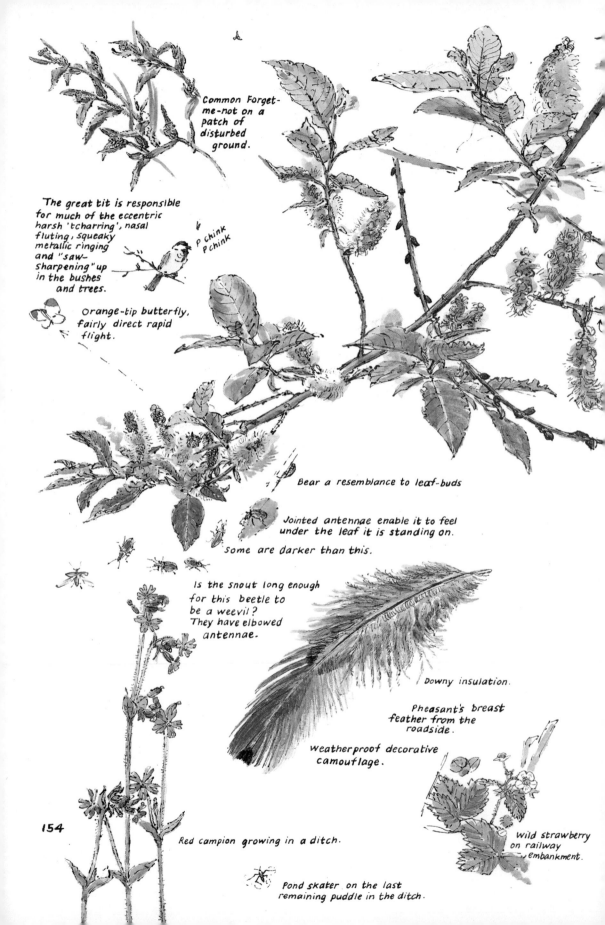

Common Forget-me-not on a patch of disturbed ground.

The great tit is responsible for much of the eccentric harsh 'tcharring', nasal fluting, squeaky metallic ringing and "saw-sharpening" up in the bushes and trees.

P chink
P chink

Orange-tip butterfly, fairly direct rapid flight.

Bear a resemblance to leaf-buds

Jointed antennae enable it to feel under the leaf it is standing on.

Some are darker than this.

Is the snout long enough for this beetle to be a weevil? They have elbowed antennae.

Downy insulation.

Pheasant's breast feather from the roadside.

weatherproof decorative camouflage.

154

Red campion growing in a ditch.

Wild strawberry on railway embankment.

Pond skater on the last remaining puddle in the ditch.

Along the edge of the wood there is a disused
railway which has been adapted as a footpath,
a very long and narrow nature reserve.

Pencaitland

Lothian, May

The goat willow (also called great sallow or pussy
willow) was covered with white fluffy seeds which
floated in the air when it was sunny.
  Another willow bush I saw later was also covered
in white; caterpillars feeding on the leaves had
covered every branch with web-like tents.

May blossom of
the hawthorn.

SPINNING
THREADS ON MY
PEN AS I DREW

Broom in
blossom.

The Tweed at Berwick
Northumberland   May

The fishermen and their tractor were able
to get out to the island through the shallow
water on the inside of the bend. They
were pulling in a long net but
didn't seem to be catching
many salmon.

One of the hedge
sparrows was
tail-quivering.

Sycamore, from the
shelter of the road bridge.

Ragged rain clouds over south Berwick.

I found an overhang out of the rain but I was dive-bombed by fulmars — quite intimidating. I was glad they had to veer away before the overhang as I've heard that they have a habit of vomiting an oily substance at you if they feel threatened. I could hear their bleating voices on the ledge above me. They had a croaking chuckle, a voice like Mr Punch in a Punch and Judy show. I think they were just perching, not nesting.

The swans wings' swished as they took off heavily and flew through one of the arches of the railway bridge.

White dead-nettle and ribwort plantain in the open wood overlooking the Tweed.

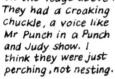

Brimstone moth

Herb Bennet or Wood Avens which I found in seed at Shaftesbury last October.

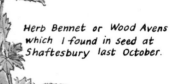

I think this rotund creature is a kind of Leaf beetle — there are over 250 species in the British Isles.

Germander speedwell

157

Alder overhanging the river.
Cones

The Tweed at Peebles

Borders region June

Alder fly

Caddis

A Daddy-long-legs
was bending its
abdomen as if to lay
eggs in the riverside
mud.

Creeping buttercup; the
middle lobe of the leaf has
a stalk (the meadow
buttercup doesn't).

There are rafts of water crowfoot
in the slower shallows of the river.
There was a mass of finely divided
underwater leaves but I couldn't see
one of the floating buttercup leaves
which water crowfoots often have.

158

On a rock at the riverside the empty case of
a creeper, the nymphal stage of a stonefly.
The adult fly has emerged from the outer skin
of the nymph. Adaptions for the nymphs
underwater life include a fringe of bristly hairs
along segments of the legs to assist swimming
and a pose as if it is doing press-ups, to
resist drag in flowing water. I wondered if
the twin tails were a form of snorkel, but
apparently they are covered in sensory hairs

Comfrey, dock, creeping thistle, creeping
buttercup, a willow herb and a yellow
mustard-type plant; all of them plants
of disturbed or cultivated ground, what
some would call rank vegetation. Plants
that move in quickly to tap the freshly
exposed supply of elements. The river
is exceptionally low at the moment but
when it floods these shingle banks must
inundated with silt full of plant nutrients.

159

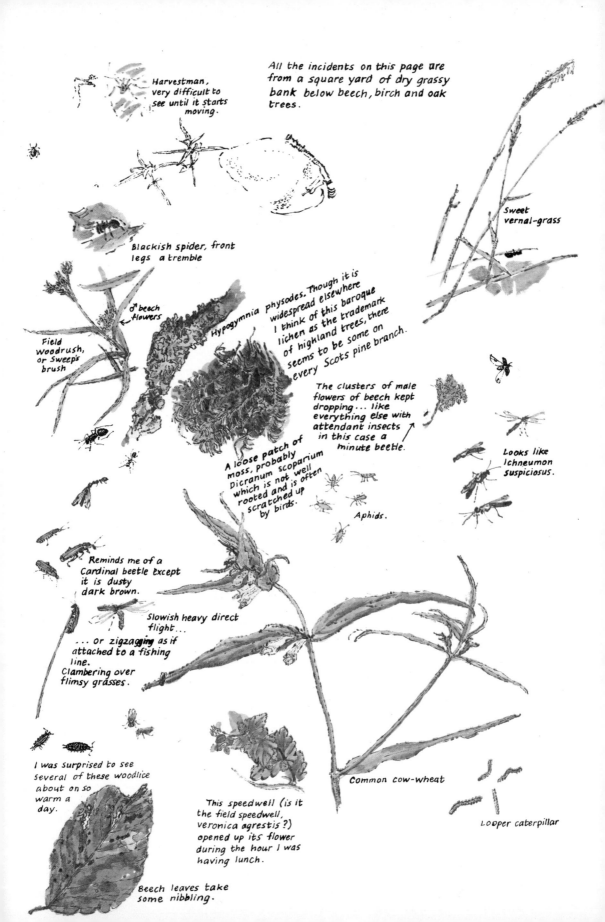

Harvestman, very difficult to see until it starts moving.

All the incidents on this page are from a square yard of dry grassy bank below beech, birch and oak trees.

Sweet vernal-grass

Blackish spider, front legs a tremble

♂ beech flowers

Field Woodrush, or Sweep's brush

Hypogymnia physodes. Though it is widespread elsewhere I think of this baroque lichen as the trademark of highland trees, there seems to be some on every Scots pine branch.

The clusters of male flowers of beech kept dropping... like everything else with attendant insects in this case a minute beetle.

Looks like Ichneumon suspiciosus.

A loose patch of moss, probably Dicranum scoparium which is not well rooted and is often scratched up by birds.

Aphids.

Reminds me of a Cardinal beetle except it is dusty dark brown.

Slowish heavy direct flight...

... or zigzagging as if attached to a fishing line. Clambering over flimsy grasses.

I was surprised to see several of these woodlice about on so warm a day.

This speedwell (is it the field speedwell, veronica agrestis?) opened up its flower during the hour I was having lunch.

Common cow-wheat

Looper caterpillar

Beech leaves take some nibbling.

Flying in morning sunlight, the Brimstone moth, the yellow pigment in its wings is fluorescent in ultraviolet light.

Great spotted woodpecker nest-hole in dead silver birch, sheltered by the bracket fungus Fomes fomentarius which is almost entirely restricted to birch in the Scottish highlands.
A chirruping chirping from inside. Two adults bringing food and leaving with droppings.

Pair of goldfinches in dispute with chaffinch.

Roe deer by the lane.

A dor beetle trundled across the path moving its legs in a ponderous clockwork sequence.

Pass of Killiecrankie
Perthshire, June
I might have spent another day observing the square yard of ground but there were heavy thunderstorms so I drew the view from the National Trust for Scotland visitor centre. The river became opaque after the heavy rain.

A gull had found a stranded salmon, almost as big as itself.

This year's birds ousted the old birds in April. They have left the old pine that has been the nest site for twenty-odd years and built in a nearby tree. The old tree has been on its last legs for years.

Cuckoo mobbed by pipits. There was a cuckoo calling at 3·00 this morning.

Bigger than the male with more of a crest ♀

♂ stretching

The male brought in a magnificent 16" rainbow trout.

RSPB LOCH GARTEN
RESERVE
June

Buzzard crossed the track continued low through the trees and glided off above the hill

The male is smaller sleeker and usually wears his crest slicked down.

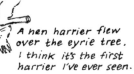

A hen harrier flew over the eyrie tree. I think it's the first harrier I've ever seen.

Short-eared owl quartering open ground to the left of the eyrie tree.

This is the view that becom[es] imprinted on your brain aft[er] a couple of days osprey wardening. The eyrie is on t[op] of the branchy tree to the le[ft;] the old, all but dead, tree on [the] right is the old nest site.

with cheek pouches stuffed he looked like a wombat

This squirrel was the perfect model he crouched there with a cone (?) for 10 minutes.

"They'll moulder away and be like other loam."
says Edwin Muir, describing tractors, in his poem 'The Horses'

This lorry was mouldering away on a hillside near Loch Garten, some kind of Cladonia lichen on the massive chassis springs, moss on the wheel rim, willow, bracken and heather were growing about it.

On the way up here I picked up a new species; a deer tick had its mouthparts firmly embedded in my leg, its body was swollen up like a tiny red match-head.

I assume it was a deer tick as there are so many roe deer about. I disturbed a doe with its fawn which was stripy, reddish brown and sandy. They bounded noiselessly through tall heather into the trees and then there was a loud throaty barking.

On my way back down the track I tucked my trousers into my socks, just in case there were any more ticks about.

Violet ground beetle

CUCK - CUCK - CUCK - CUCKOO
Changing its tune

Thursday morning
5 AM

Only a small
brown trout
— about 9"
this morning.

← ROE
DEER

An enormous capercaillie
cock made a dignified
progress through
the heather.

The two young were just begining
to show their heads. A third egg
failed to hatch.

In 1967 there were three pairs of ospreys
nesting in Scotland, the following year,
when I first came here as a voluntary
warden, there were seven pairs. Now
there are over 20 pairs, in 1979 thirty
young were reared.

164

It took several mornings and afternoons, in between working as a warden on the osprey reserve, to draw the decaying lorry. There was an ant motorway along a twenty yard stretch of the overgrown forest track. In the mornings the traffic was almost entirely outwards from the nest, at midday there was fairly equal two-way movement and in the late afternoon most of the ants were on their way back.

It was so busy near the nest I had to sit fifteen or twenty feet away to make a drawing. An elderly couple coming by warned me not to stay where I was in case the ants got me.

The nest of the wood ant, about three feet across, built of pine needles and twigs, domed so that rain rolls off.

the Bottleneck nest.

Northern Marsh Orchid ?

The pupa are shaped like fat white cigars.

Cladonia fimbriata, golf tee shaped.

Cladonia gracilis

Moss capsules

wood ant

This lichen, Cladonia floerkeana, is known, appropriately, as Devil's matches.

While walking down the hill with my osprey warden team-mates John and Sue I saw a broken bottle in the field near the road. When I picked it up to take it back to camp I found there was an ants' nest inside it. The neck of the bottle was stuffed with moss and there were white pupae, "ants' eggs", inside. John picked up a piece of zinc which was lying close by to cover the bottle. But under the zinc was another nest of the same species of ant. We carefully put the bottle and zinc back in place. The ants under the sheet of metal evidently had an unsettled existence. Two yellowed squares nearby in the grass showed where the zinc had been picked up and cast down on previous occasions.

A keen amateur ant-man I met later suggested that the bottle might have been a solarium. He told me that ants bring pupae nearer the surface during the day and take them down into the nest in the evening. The glass must have given an extreme greenhouse-effect. 165

Castle Douglas
June

Floors loch lies in a hollow amongst drumlins.
Drumlins are low hills with an egg-shaped profile
composed of material dumped by glaciers.
They were probably shaped by flowing ice,
in this case flowing into the nearby Solway Firth,
as dunes are formed by wind and ripple marks
by the tide.

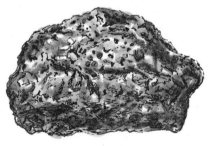

Tufted duck

A pair of redshank
3 noisy oystercatchers
Swallows skimming the pool.
3 duck (mallard?)

The soils of sandy
pebbly glacial debris
seem to suit beech,
there are some
magnificent trees
by the lane and on
the slopes of the
drumlins.

Piece of granite which I picked up at the trackside.
Masses of granite were intruded into the local rocks
some 400 million years ago. At this time two continental
plates were colliding, Scotland was part of the North
American plate, England part of the European. As the
drifting continents came together the ocean between
was squeezed out of existence and sediments and rocks
were compressed. The enormous pressures involved caused
the melting which led to the formation of the granite.

166

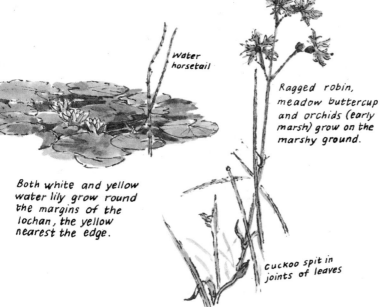

Water horsetail

Both white and yellow water lily grow round the margins of the lochan, the yellow nearest the edge.

Ragged robin, meadow buttercup and orchids (early marsh) grow on the marshy ground.

Cuckoo spit in joints of leaves

merou argle argle argle

THE EFFECTS OF MOOING & SCRATCHING YOUR CHIN AT THE SAME TIME.

I wish you could hear the sounds too; the bullocks scrunching about in the reeds, the extensive and vigorous bathing routine of the swan.

Work was interrupted by the arrival of a group of frisky heifers and one stocky friendly bull.

Also the first version of this landscape got washed off the page by a heavy shower. I had been trying to 'float' on the grey sky in watercolour.

167

Gourock
on the Clyde , June

Amongst the shore life the almost inevitable polite and friendly drunk.
"Are you a geologist?.."   "Oh, no.."
"You're an anthropologist?"   "No.."
"You _must_ be a geologist."
"No I'm an illustrator. I do drawings."
"Do you know "The Gleaners" draw me that."
"Well. I've got to do some drawings for a book."
"Give me some paper, I'll draw you!"

Curled dock on rocks, steps and concrete along the shore.

Another species was a black Scottie called Jock. Just, as a matter of course, putting his leg up against my haversack.
"Push him away!" called his mistress "he's no respecter of people!"

I had to keep wetting this pebble to make the pattern show up. It is a hard metamorphic rock, lighter bands are intruded into it at all angles.

168

The three young were smaller and more stripy.

The female eider had a definite speculum.

whisky bottle bobbing along the shore.

Brown rats were rustling noisily amongst the cans and cartons between the boulders. This one looked quite charming but a larger one I saw later had a more piratical look about it.

A bed of harder rock caps and overhangs more easily eroded layers. These rocks are laced with intruded veins (of quartz?) which stand proud of the surface.

169

Rannoch Moor
July

Although you can see for miles in all directions there is a feeling of being hemmed in. The moor is ringed about by mountains. In the Ice Age this was a centre from which huge glaciers gouged their ways along the glens that radiate from here taking chunks of Rannoch Moor granite with them.

By ten thousand years ago the ice had melted leaving hummocks of debris over the moor. But it was not until three thousand years ago that pine forest became established here. Since then the climate has become wetter and the roots of this ancient forest lie buried in the peat.

A water vole swam and scrambled nimbly through the roots and under the bank. Its fur was much darker than those we have at home, exactly the same colour as peat in fact.

It is so quiet on the moor: not even sheep, there are skylarks singing, snipe drumming, gulls calling, the occasional train or plane. You can hear the rain approaching a couple of miles away. A weird sound.

Bog myrtle or sweet gale (which I also drew at Wicken Fen). I'm addicted to the fragrance of the crushed leaves. Also there was deer-sedge, bog asphodel, heather, cross-leaved heath, bell heather, sphagnum moss and a 'Reindeer moss' lichen, Cladonia impexa.

Suilven
Sutherland July

The extraordinary shape of Suilven stands out like a child's version of what a mountain should be like. It is a remnant of Torridonian sandstone resting on a knobbly landscape of more ancient and harder Lewisian gneiss. Next day it had its head in the clouds and looked like the Breughel painting of the tower of Babel.

An erratic boulder of Torridonian sandstone lay on the side of a knoll. This is the same material that for Suilven. It was coarse textured wi gritty layers. It lay on top of anot piece (perhaps part of the same bou which was so packed with gravel t it resembled the pebble-dash used on house wall

Large white butterflies in mating flight.

While drawing bog asphodel I noticed what looked like a largish moss capsule. It was the un-opened flower-bud of sundew. No wonder I haven't seen them before; having seen close-up film of them catching insects I imagined them to be as big as Venus fly-traps. But this spider-like rosette of tiny soup-spoon-shaped leaves would have fitted on the face of my wrist-watch. There were a dozen plants on the square foot of wet mossy ground by me.

glistening filaments cling to leaf of a sedge

Spreading over the rock to form a hard, dense covering. Reminds me of blackthorn. Could it be a sort of cotoneaster? It can't be Diapensia known from only one hill-top in Inverness-shire. I'll guess at Scottish sandwort, which could well be growing here, fairly close to sea in a bare stony place.

Lewisian gneiss, a hard rock with small shining flakes (of mica?) in it. Even this fragment shows the way it cracks along lines running at angles to the grain. These cracks are weaknesses caused by tremendous pressures which have acted on the rock since it was laid down over 2,700 million years ago. The original layers of this crystalline rock are so compressed and changed that they have a uniform hardness and no longer erode at different rates.

Some of the outcrops are like twisted variegated toffee or warped swiss rolls. The pattern in this rock reminds me of carvings of Celtic beasts.

172

Growing in a crevice, English stonecrop which grows along the western coasts of England, Ireland and Scotland. It has fleshy succulent leaves.

One exposure of gneiss, steeper than a house roof, had the cracks and wrinkles, the colour and texture of elephant skin. I couldn't resist climbing up it. At the base were big black lumps the size of footballs set into the rockface. The lumps were from another sediment — the strata lines went at different angles to the rock it was embedded in.

Moss colonises this exposure of gneiss by following the grid of cracks.

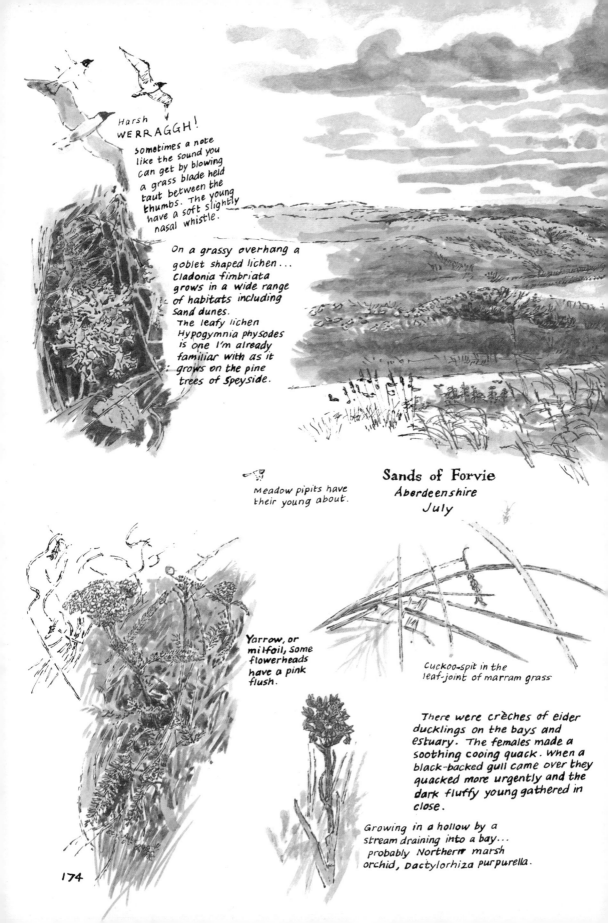

Harsh
WERRAGGH!
Sometimes a note
like the sound you
can get by blowing
a grass blade held
taut between the
thumbs. The young
have a soft slightly
nasal whistle.

On a grassy overhang a
goblet shaped lichen...
Cladonia fimbriata
grows in a wide range
of habitats including
sand dunes.
The leafy lichen
Hypogymnia physodes
is one I'm already
familiar with as it
grows on the pine
trees of Speyside.

Meadow pipits have
their young about.

Sands of Forvie
Aberdeenshire
July

Yarrow, or
milfoil, some
flowerheads
have a pink
flush.

Cuckoo-spit in the
leaf-joint of marram grass

There were crèches of eider
ducklings on the bays and
estuary. The females made a
soothing cooing quack. When a
black-backed gull came over they
quacked more urgently and the
dark fluffy young gathered in
close.

Growing in a hollow by a
stream draining into a bay...
probably Northern marsh
orchid, Dactylorhiza purpurella.

174

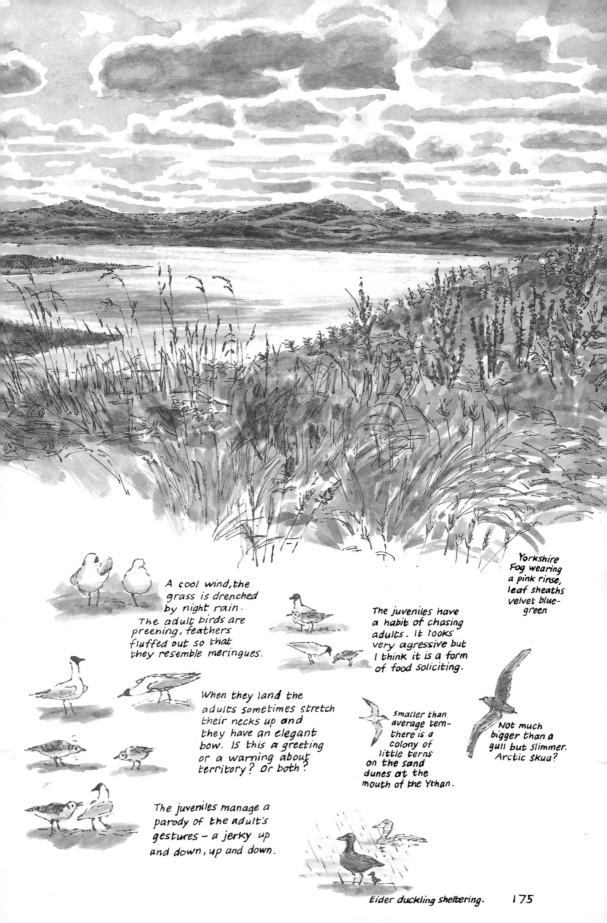

A cool wind, the grass is drenched by night rain. The adult birds are preening, feathers fluffed out so that they resemble meringues.

Yorkshire Fog wearing a pink rinse, leaf sheaths velvet blue-green

The juveniles have a habit of chasing adults. It looks very agressive but I think it is a form of food soliciting.

When they land the adults sometimes stretch their necks up and they have an elegant bow. Is this a greeting or a warning about territory? Or both?

smaller than average tern - there is a colony of little terns on the sand dunes at the mouth of the Ythan.

Not much bigger than a gull but slimmer. Arctic skua?

The juveniles manage a parody of the adult's gestures - a jerky up and down, up and down.

Eider duckling sheltering.

175

Jackdaws nest in the tall wych elms. There'd not be much left of this wood if the elms disappeared — and one elm has died completely already.

A hoverfly settled on my thumb-nail while I was drawing.
Blow-flies bask on lumps of rock amongst the grass.

Rabbits that had been feeding along the edge of the field ran back to the wood as I approached.
A small one attempted to compress itself into the ground and I only noticed it when I was two feet from it.

Jackdaws called in alarm and one of the rabbits stood up on its hind-legs to see what the danger was.

176

Corbridge
Northumberland, July

Sphagnum peat and dune sands are all very well, but when it comes to getting your boots muddy you can't beat the dark earth. This patch of woodland breathes earthiness of an evening. I enjoyed the spectacular scenery of Scotland but there is more than enough to keep me occupied, watching and drawing, along this field edge. For me this is almost home territory, an "ordinary" sort of place. Yet no place is all that ordinary; there is a Roman road a couple of fields away and, according to the geological map of Northern Britain the wood lies close to a geological boundary, a tongue of millstone grit outcrops on this hillside over rocks of the Carboniferous limestone series.

Someone had been shooting the previous evening. I think the victim was a young jackdaw. Feathers in the grass stood up like rabbit's ears.

177

CREEPING
THISTLE

Terrington
North Yorkshire
July

When someone talks about countryside this is the landscape that comes to my mind. Rolling hills and hollows, copses and hedgerows, scattered farms; mixed farms with cattle in one field and potatoes in the **next** or barley rippling in the wind. Lanes, rutted tracks and footpaths to explore.

My father used to come shooting here, and fishing at the dam which lies behind those trees on the left. There is a tendency to develop a romantic image of a place you knew as a child and when you go back you find it is somehow shrunken and you'd forgotten there were all those pylons. I haven't been back here for over 15 years but the place is as pleasant as I remember it.

Our springer spaniel used to become excited and he'd start whining as soon as the car started bumping down the last bit of unmade track, anticipating all the trails he'd sniff out amongst the fields and woods. Partridge were his speciality. In fact it seemed that anticipation was the part he enjoyed the most because as he got older he was all for getting back into the car after a quick reconnoitre.

Lesser burdock

Chicory, growing amongst
tall grasses and hogweed,
had flowers which
seemed a purer blue
than they actually were.

The fly had such big
feet that I could hear
its footsteps as it
walked about the
page.

"Flies of the British
Isles" tells me that Sarcophaga
flesh flies are renowned for their
big feet, also they have a stripy
thorax, mosaic-effect abdomen
and eyes which are bright red
when the creature is alive.

Enormous old sycamore
which had died back
completely. 179

HOME AGAIN

My journey has brought me full circle back to my own doorstep while the year too has turned from July to July. This has been an ideal starting point as well as a base camp from which to explore Britain. Here in Wakefield we are just about on the diagonal line that separates highland and lowland Britain. To the north and west lie the ancient, contorted rocks of mountain and moorland, while to the south and east younger, softer rocks form scarps and downland.

A visit to the wilder side of Britain always brings home to me how drab and despoiled many parts of the lowlands are. Origins and structure, so obvious in highland Britain, are often obscured beneath concrete, brick and tarmac. But even in the most built-up areas it is possible to observe wildlife and get beneath the layers of human activity. The buildings themselves may be constructed of limestone crammed with fossils, or of once-molten granites.

Looking through these pages I realise what an extraordinary experience it has been to see so much of this country in so short a period. I am left with so many vivid images and impressions, yet I feel I am only just beginning to get to know Britain. This book shows no more than a slice through time; there is so much I should still like to see. In particular I would like to go back to some of the places I've drawn here and see them in different seasons.

'Why don't you finish that drawing indoors?' my sister asked me as I set off between showers of rain to try and complete the page of seeding willow at Pencaitland. 'You're so dependent on the weather.' I do seem to have made life difficult for myself in the past year, but I would have missed so much if I hadn't spent as long out in the open. In the far north I've crouched among ice-scarred boulders to draw insect-eating plants in a peat bog; on a concrete roof in London I found an ants' nest. I've sheltered in Merlin's Cave at Tintagel when winter gales lashed the Cornish coast and on a day when the fens of East Anglia shimmered under a sweltering sun I was chased a quarter of a mile by a persistent horse-fly.

There were many close encounters with wildlife, some all too close – the fulmars that dive-bombed me with menacing enthusiasm at Berwick could have auditioned for an Alfred Hitchcock film. And if I hadn't been out in the field I would have missed the seal that swam lazily into Crab Bay, the red kite chasing a raven over Tregaron Bog, foxes playing tag at dusk below Headon Warren, the butterflies, bees and hoverflies that were attracted to the bright colours in my paintbox, and the weasels and stoats hunting in woods and hedges.

Such unexpected incidents help to make a day in the country exciting, but if a five-star rarity fails to turn up I don't feel I've wasted my time. I am not a train spotter; I'm not desperate to tick off species on a list. At Selborne, for example, I saw nothing that was particularly rare, but the variety of plants, insects and animals that I did come across made this a pleasant place to explore. And sometimes it is not the individual incidents I remember so much as the overall feeling of being there. The lonely desolation of Rannoch had a deep effect on me and I tried to put this across in the watercolour.

So these drawings bring back to me what it felt like to be there, the flavour, the texture, sounds and smells of a particular place. I get foot weary treading city pavements and I'm always glad to get out into the country. In the Highlands, for instance, every step is different to the last – spongy sphagnum moss, soft carpets of pine-needles, crinkled exposures of bare rock, knee-deep heather and shoulder-high bracken. Streams are pure and sparkling or slightly peaty. A Highland pinewood has a clean, damp smell and its own atmosphere of natural sound.

At the end of a year I am left with the impression that the surface of this island is a complex, ever-changing tapestry. The countryside may appear to be static but really it is in continual change. Already the dunes at Forvie will have drifted into slightly different shapes. The reedbeds will have extended a little farther into Martham Broad. Springheads erode the steep slopes of the Devil's Punch Bowl.

But alongside these natural forms of change come changes made by man. Every part of the country I visited had some kind of threat hanging over it. I saw hedges being grubbed up, oil pollution on beaches and on the Welsh coast a nuclear power station, nearing the end of its career, that will be deadly to all forms of life for years to come. On balance Britain is becoming less green and pleasant; but there is still a continual tension between man and nature. Motorways may chew up farmland, cut through hillsides and bisect woods, but their extensive verges dotted with thorn and gorse are now a favourite hunting ground for kestrels – I saw eight on a single motorway journey.

In fact, some of the most rewarding places I visited were those where there was an interaction between man and nature. The brickpits at Peterborough were surprisingly rich in wildlife, and I found more than enough to draw along a canal in Birmingham and a stretch of derelict railway near Macclesfield. Waste and dereliction may be appalling, but such scenes contain possibilities of their own that it would be a pity to overlook. A decaying lorry on a hillside in Scotland, in a metamorphosis between mechanical and organic, proved to be a fascinating subject to draw.

Greed, selfishness and loutish behaviour seem to make the majority of news stories, so much so that it is surprising that 99 per cent of the people I've met have not only been kind and helpful but have gone out of their way to help. Travellers' tales of foreign parts tell of countries where courtesy and hospitality are still a tradition. Unlikely as it seems this is true of Britain. Of course there is that one per cent who are bad-tempered, rude or surly, but we all have our off days and such people more often add a touch of comic relief than cause anybody, except perhaps themselves, any actual distress.

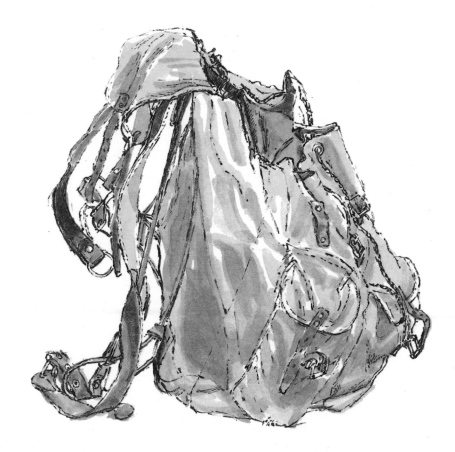

INDEX OF PLACES

INDEX OF SPECIES

Y